MW00325825

So Much Depends Upon...

An Anthology

So Much Depends Upon…

An Anthology

Written and Edited by
The Red Wheelbarrow Writers

Bellingham, Washington / 2018

Penchant Press International

So Much Depends Upon...
An Anthology

Copyright © 2018 Cami Ostman

All rights reserved. No part of this publication may be repro-
duced, distributed or transmitted in any form or by any
means, including photocopying, recording, digital scanning,
or other electronic or mechanical methods, without the prior
written permission of the publisher, except in the case of brief
quotations embodied in critical reviews and certain other
noncommercial uses permitted by copyright law, and with
the exception of individual contributors who retain all rights
to their own work herein. For permission requests, please
contact Penchant Press International, LLC.

1st Edition

Printed in the United States of America

Penchant Press International, LLC
P.O. Box 1333
Blaine, WA 98231
Penchantpressinternational.com

Library of Congress Control Number: 2018945208

ISBN 978-0-9724960-3-2

Ostman, Cami 1967 –
So Much Depends Upon…
An Anthology

Cover Photography: Jolene Hanson
Cover Design: J. Allen Fielder

So much depends
upon

a red wheel
barrow

glazed with rain
water

beside the white
chickens.

William Carlos Williams
"XXII" from *Spring and All* (1923)

A Short History of Red Wheelbarrow Writers
and its namesake poem, "XXII"

On a regular kind of Northwest Saturday in 2012—sunless and damp—I hurried from my inconvenient, four-blocks-away parking space to the Pickford Film Center where a nascent group of writers was meeting in the lobby. Laura Kalpakian, my teacher for "Memory into Memoir," a three-semester offering through Western Washington University Extension, encouraged her students to attend a monthly Happy Hour for support.

I was late. I looked through the wide windows and saw a half-dozen women, already in deep discussion, seated around two pushed-together tables. Several held wineglasses, some munched popcorn. How could I enter this scene without being conspicuous, apologetic, and awkward? I walked back to my car, vowing to attend the next month . . . and to arrive early.

* * *

Since December 2012, I have been a regular member of Red Wheelbarrow Writers, a loose affiliation of working writers who produce independently, and who join together to support, encourage, and sustain one another.

As such, I've tried out current compositions at Happy Hours, practiced fiction writing by contributing to Red Wheelbarrow's annual collective novel for National Novel Writing Month, and increased productivity at Write-Out gatherings in myriad locations. I've been "on display" at Village Books' WRITERS IN THE WINDOW, read my work at the same bookstore, and jumped into RWB's version of National Poetry Writing Month. I've participated in online workshops, discussed books at a monthly book club, been inspired by Whatcom Memoir Writing Month, and contributed to the group's first publication *Memory into Memoir*.

That is a whopping list of ten ways that Red Wheelbarrow Writers has enriched my own life. It doesn't count parties, spin-off critique groups, and association with new friends—intelligent, curious, word-driven writers. And so, as a grateful beneficiary, I have delegated to myself the twin tasks of summarizing the short history of Red Wheelbarrow Writers and providing background on the poem from whose name the organization was derived.

In early 2010, three writers—Cami Ostman, Susan Tive, and Laura Kalpakian—were conducting writing workshops at the Chrysalis Inn on a diversity of topics. They hosted well-known contributors to the Northwest's literary scene: Brooke Warner of Seal Press; Elizabeth Wales, Seattle literary agent; and Gary Luke, editor-publisher of Sasquatch Books.

"What we found by doing the workshops," Susan said, "was that writers really enjoyed the networking and support during the happy hour at the end of the sessions." They decided to form a group.

Laura took on the challenge of finding a name, certain that there would be something in Walt Whitman, but she couldn't find a phrase that would stand on its own. Too much death, she thought. Too much death as well as she skimmed through Emily Dickinson, Whitman's contemporary and opposite. "Hart Crane, too obscure. Eliot, too cerebral. Ditto Ezra Pound. Besides he went wonky and Fascist. Langston Hughes, too much underlying melancholy. Marianne Moore? A bit prim."

Then she remembered William Carlos Williams, the focus of a class she'd taken during her doctoral studies at the University of California, San Diego. Much of his work was "short, aphoristic, oblique." She suggested the first two lines of *The Red Wheelbarrow* ("So much depends / upon") to Susan and Cami, who completed Williams' beginning lines with *community*.

* * *

The poem that we know as *The Red Wheelbarrow* first appeared, identified only as a number, "XXII" in William Carlos Williams' book *Spring and All*, published in 1923 by his friend Robert McAlmon, in a limited print run of three hundred copies in Paris.

In 2012, the Library of Congress singled out *Spring and All* as one of eighty-eight books that "shaped America." Librarian of Congress James Billington explained that the purpose was not to catalog "best books," but "to identify works by American writers that influenced our lives and to spark conversation." *The Red Wheelbarrow* poem has sparked conversation and analysis over the last ninety-five years.

The poem also has sparked the creation of an action-oriented, supportive community for writers. Laura points out, "One of Cami's great gifts is the ability to create community. She brought that special gift to bear on the early workshops we presented and she brings it to what has become Red Wheelbarrow Writers."

Susan has moved to Oregon and Cami now lives in Seattle—both stay in touch. Cami continues to be the emcee for Happy Hours, keeps the website supplied with fresh content, and encourages the cadre of three hundred Facebook followers to participate in Red Wheelbarrow's initiatives. Many others have contributed to the vitality of Red Wheelbarrow Writers. To mention one, Jessica H. Stone (Jes), the co-owner of Penchant Press International. Like Robert McAlmon who published his friends William Carlos Williams, Ezra Pound, Nathanael West, Gertrude Stein, and Ernest Hemingway, Jes provided the resources of her publishing company to bring *Memory into Memoir* and *So Much Depends Upon . . .* to the marketplace.

Of William Carlos Williams' poem, Laura admits, "I was not absolutely delighted with using the line for our title at first, but now I *am* delighted with it and with how Red Wheelbarrow Writers has turned out, and continues to evolve."

Take a cue from Laura: read this anthology of memoir and memoir-based fiction, each of which completes the idea of *So Much Depends Upon . . .* Delight and insight will be yours.

Linda Q. Lambert
Bellingham, WA
June 2018
redwheelbarrowwriters.com
facebook.com/redwheelbarrowwriters

Table of Contents

Acknowledgments

The Whole Story

Nancy Adair and Jeffrey Adair

Nancy

Was it fair to drag an eighth-grader and a fourth-grader to the heart of darkness, where even in 1990 we communicated by shortwave radio as family 151? Living a normal life was a challenge, but my sons had more resilience and creativity than I ever knew. Until now.

* * *

KRRRRRK "Dispatch."

"This is 151 Alpha. Please connect me with 225 Sierra. Over."

"Come back, 151!"

"Hi. My Delta 1 and Delta 2 request your Delta 2 and Delta 3 for a sleepover at our residence tonight. Over."

"Message received, 151! I will deliver Delta 2 and 3 after lunch. Over."

"Lima Charlie!" (Loud and Clear.) "Over and out."

Jeff

Alpha communicated. Sierra facilitated. Deltas activated. The party was on!

I lived in the Congo during the crumbling years of Mobutu Sese Seko's dictatorship, at a time when enemies at the border plotted the inevitable coup. But months before Kabila's rebel army marched into the capital, another battle would send my corner of Kinshasa up in smoke.

Behind razor-wired walls, my older brother and I passed our happy little lives within the friendly confines of U.S. Embassy housing. Regardless of the chaos outside, Mason, aka "the director," and I did what normal kids did on school vacations during the VHS camcorder revolution—we made movies, epic action-adventures with titles like *Spy Chaser* and *Crocodile Jeffrey*.

Our tropical compound, with its large yard, pool, and hibiscus bushes provided a vast stage for an army of G.I. Joe action figures. With analog AV technology and stop-action production skills, we sent G.I. Joe on myriad clichéd adventures. Save the girl, disarm the bomb, bust the druggies. And we always added a catchphrase like "I'll be back!"

Once the 225 Deltas, aka Roman and Durham, arrived at our residence, the director discussed his concept. Compromise gave us the title, *The 13 Dirty Dozen Dudes*. Yes, it still needed "workshopping," particularly for bad alliteration and fuzzy math.

As is often the case with "on-location shoots," the elements became an issue. Congo was known for Biblical plagues, particularly when it came to insects. We dug miniature trenches on our tropical set, but just as the director called, "Action!" giant leafcutter ants swarmed our entire three-inch army and added a sci-fi element we were not prepared for. The director yelled, "Cut!" and we scriptwriters returned to the notepad.

Because of the infestation, we relocated the filming indoors. Fortunately, we had already captured enough footage of boot camp. Given the arduous nature of a stop-action production, we made the creative decision to jump from the opening scene to the finale. Plot development died on my bedroom floor.

Nancy

When I came home from work, I was impressed to find the four Deltas scattered around Jeff's bedroom, all immersed in scriptwriting. Admiring the industry of these kids, I lingered in the hall and then leaned on the doorframe to watch. Until it crunched. Until my shoulder poked right through the stiff enamel paint. I jabbed up and down, only to find that the frame no longer existed. Carpenter ants had eaten all the wood. The house, like the country, crumbled around us.

Jeff

After scripting the final attack, a winter scene in an "alpine lair," we needed props. How might we create snow in the Congo? We raided the linen closet finding two crisp white sheets for tundra and tiny-blue-flowered sheets for our "winter lily patch."

Nurturing our talent, the director let Roman, Durham, and me choreograph and narrate our own "fight scenes." Roman's was a knock-down-drag-out brawl finishing with a Karate Kid crane move. Mine consisted of a drug deal gone bad followed by a flurry of gunfire between my hero, Duke, and the big, bad Sanchez gang.

After dinner, the director pulled moving boxes from storage. With scissors and glue, we settled in the living room to watch a video while we created our new set pieces.

Nancy

After dinner, I checked on the boys. A videotape of *Red Dawn* played on the TV. The fledgling filmmakers were half-watching the movie, half-designing the set, and fully immersed in creativity.

Outside, our two security guards darted past our wall of glass doors. My heart stopped. Were they chasing an intruder? No. They were chasing dinner. It was termite season again. With their own creativity, the guards used a T-shirt to net the flying ants attracted to our security lights. They ate several at once. Now and then, a guard walked right up to our windows because the reflection helped him locate a termite wing stuck between his teeth.

"Would it be rude of me to shut the drapes?" I asked the boys.

"Yes," Mason said. "Leave them open. We're okay."

Jeff

By ten o'clock, my bedroom was turned into an alpine hideout fit for a Bond villain. The set featured a built-to-scale cardboard compound for exterior shots. Detail was important. The cutaway of the evil empire's lair showed the kingpin's desk. Behind it hung "scale portraits," magazine clippings of villains like Stalin and Hans Gruber.

Filming resumed.

The stop-action technique was time-consuming. It used action figures or Claymation to ever so slightly move each character so that the amalgam of still pictures rendered a moving image. The final attack scene took hours to shoot, even though the whole war would unfold in an eight-minute video.

Nancy

When I awoke, the boys were already up and filming. It warmed my heart. I would no longer beat myself up for being the bad mother who moved her kids to a life of deprivation: no TV, no Cineplex, no Chuck E. Cheese. To my delight, deprivation ignited their resourcefulness. Now, I thought, look at these clever Deltas. Maybe I'm the mother of the year!

"See you tonight after our tennis tournament," I said and left the boys in the gentle care of Sanda, our male nanny/cleaner/cook.

Jeff

Henchmen bit the dust in deadly shoot-outs, complete with elaborate bullet holes. In the final confrontation, Sergeant Slaughter chased the big Boss into an A-framed Swiss chalet with a pitched roof made from our Monopoly board.

"Can we use my tank in the last scene?" Roman asked. "Can we blow a hole in the building?"

"I love it!" cried the director. "We can use toilet paper for the smoke from the tank and then . . . and then, let's cut a mortar hole in the cardboard and burn around the edges!"

"O . . . kay," Durham said, unsure about the burn part.

But we did it! The tank rolled in by stop-action. The captain commanded, "He went into headquarters! Let's bomb him out!"

Booooom! roared the tank as the director zoomed in on plumes of double-ply Charmin smoke. We stopped the action, cut a hole in the building, and the director burned its outline to make the hideout look like scorched earth.

The camera rolled. Smoke billowed through the hole. As the flames tempered, victorious soldiers cheered. Suddenly, the smoke increased. The flames had rekindled. Fire poured out of the box. A raging inferno consumed the chalet—and my room.

With the camera still rolling, the barefoot director jumped into the scene, landing on the Monopoly board and crashing down on the Swiss chalet. His move shot ash and flames at the camera lens. Pure action magic! Cool enough to make Jerry Bruckheimer swoon.

We finished the production and ran to the living room to preview the tape on television. Genius! All the way to the credits, which rolled in eight-bit text and listed me as the best boy. I didn't know what that meant, but it sounded great.

In the end, *The 13 Dirty Dozen Dudes* was shot over the course of twenty-four hours on a Pop-Tart budget and can only be described as a cult classic yet to be discovered.

Nancy

When my husband and I returned from work, Roman and Durham were already gone, and Jeff and Mason seemed surprised.

"I thought you were playing tennis," Mason said, removing a videotape from the VCR. "Were the mosquitos bad?"

"No," I replied. "It was worse. We thought we heard rain on the court, but it was a storm of giant rhinoceros beetles, dropping out of the sky, landing on their backs, horn side up. Players stepped on them and turned their ankles. We had to postpone."

"Too bad," Mason replied, putting the video behind his back.

"Is that your movie?" my husband said. "Let's premiere it after dinner."

"Can't." Mason said. "Still editing."

"Well, then, how about a rousing game of Monopoly?"

"Uh, not till we finish editing."

Jeff

In case you wondered, no G.I. Joes were injured in the making of this film! The linens, on the other hand . . .

The Alps took a major hit during the last battle. They were singed with ash and riddled with tiny burn holes. The quick-thinking director stuffed the snow-white tundra and winter lilies into a garbage bag. At the same time, I opened my windows and turned on the ceiling fan to air out my bedroom. Sanda took care of the scorched set.

A day later, the sheets remained charred and reeking of arson. The director dunked them in our pool to get rid of the smell. When the sheets dried, he asked me to help him disguise the evidence.

"Why can't we disappear the sheets," I asked, "like a mob informant in *The Godfather*?"

"Mom will miss them," he said. His avoidance motivation has always been strong—he'd rather hobble around on burned feet than confront our parents. That day his evasion tactics were meticulous.

"Here's the plan: we cut a square around each ash mark and burn hole. Then we fold the sheets and hide them in the back of the linen closet."

The perfect getaway plan, eh?

* * *

Cut to the Chase

Two weeks later, Mom stood at the linen closet between our rooms. "What happened to my sheets?"

I remained in my room away from the door.

"Sanda!" she called, "*venez ici, s'il vous plaît.*"

I heard the slapping of Sanda's flip-flops in the hallway and then Mom showing him the sheets. He must have shrugged because he didn't say a word. I couldn't let him take the hit. It wasn't fair. I appeared in my doorway ready to confess when Mason appeared in his.

"What's wrong, Mom?" He sounded so innocent, his acting even better than his directing.

"What in the heck happened to my sheets?"

She held one up, and the picture of her eyes framed by two square burn holes has forever seared in my memory the dark side of my normal childhood. At the same moment, I studied the artistry of a job well done. Not one scorch mark was visible.

Upset and confused, my mother asked, "What eats cotton? Termites?"

"No," Mason said, "but square-mouthed beetles probably do."

"Oh, no," she said, examining a sheet. "We have square-mouthed beetles, too? We need to move."

Mason nodded. "Indeed."

Sanda kept his job, and we lived to film another day.

Nancy's Postscript

The U.S. Embassy never let us move. I never saw the video. I never was mother of the year. And on all of these accounts, I never knew why until this writing. So much depends upon the whole story. Even more depends upon resilience and creativity.

Novelist, humorist, and travel blogger, Nancy Adair left the United States in the eighties with her diplomat husband, two babies, and an electric typewriter. The diplomatic life agreed with her. Her writing, however, goes beyond politics to the joys and absurdities of life in every little corner of the world. NancyAdair.com

A childhood overseas then a Master's Degree in African History, Jeff Adair now teaches at the International School of Bangkok, where he entertains students and teachers with the tales of his youth.

The Good Old Days

Christine Bostrom

Mom and I had lost sight of each other at our favorite antique shop, The Vintage Rabbit. I was looking at turn-of-the-century beaded purses to add to my collection. I had made my purchase and was walking through the store, when I saw her in a corner going through old Depression glass and cheap kitchen odds and ends. I wondered why she seemed to be interested in worn-out merchandise and seemingly useless, ugly objects, when there were so many beautiful antiques to choose from. As I approached her, I noticed sadness in her face.

"Mom, are you okay?"

"Oh, hi, Hon, yeah . . . You know, my mother had a pot just like this: poor, old, dull aluminum. Several times a week, she boiled navy beans or potatoes in it. It touched my heart to see it here, and brought back a rush of memories of home and how things were back then. Funny how even things you hated as a child can become a cherished part of your past."

"You're not thinking of buying it, are you? It's dented; what would you do with it now?"

My mom looked away. Tears welled up in her eighty-year-old eyes. "Yes, I am going to buy it. When we get home, I'll tell you a story."

It was a sunny, summer day. We sat outside with a glass of white wine, munching on crackers and cheese. Noisy bees and silent butterflies wove their way around the flowers. A lazy day.

"Christine, close your eyes and I'll tell you about a little girl on a day like this."

I closed my eyes and lay back against the chaise lounge. Mom began.

"She was sitting on the step, head down, a crooked stick in hand, scribbling in the dirt under her bare feet. It was spring, one of those days of first bright sunshine. With the sun came the sound of crickets, an abundance of dandelions, and every kind of weed imaginable. Tiny insects scurried this way and that across the brown earth, working or hunting or going home to their nests. The warmth felt so delicious after the cold winter, the snow covering all, and the long hours indoors. The very act of breathing became a birth of fresh new life. The feeling of free time to revel in her senses and study the lives of the small beings made her cherish her existence and nature around her.

"On the steep hill across the street, the trees and bushes were covered with buds and newborn leaves, making a greenness that hadn't been there yesterday. The sun dazed her and she felt good, relaxed and lazy. A small brown dog sprawled in the dust, feeling just as relaxed and lazy as she did. Nothing to do. Nothing but meeting new bugs, learning where every new sprout was being born. Close-up inspection: when you are small, you are very close to the earth, and your new eyes see it all for the first time. Tiny things are nearer and larger than they will ever be again. As a child, each blade of grass, each stem of a wildflower, the way the dirt moves as you trace through it with a stick, all of these are wonderful because they are the first times.

"As a cloud passed in front of the sun, cutting off the warmth, the little girl looked up. She crossed the muddy street to the hill. The dog came alive and led the way, up into a tangled, brushy world of sunshine and shadow. Suddenly, stick still in hand, feet still shoeless, she and the dog were running wildly, possessed by exuberance and pure joy. She had to run, let loose the energy of freedom. What fun it was to glide through the softness of spring, to feel toes and heels dig into the soft, warm earth! She was alive!"

I opened my eyes and saw a smile on Mom's face. She paused, eyes closed, reliving the childish pleasure of spring, nature, and freedom from the burdens of the world. Then she continued, still in storytelling mode, needing to share her reverie.

"What became of that child? Did she ever again sit in the sun, climb the hill and run through the field, each time bursting with joy? Yes, she had more springs, and she did these things again. Somehow, though, each year there was a little less freedom and a little less exuberance. Each summer, she was taller and the ground was farther away. The individual blades of grass became blurry tufts. Crickets no longer interested her; she already knew how to catch them. The pine became just a tree, rocks just rocks, and the mud, something to avoid. Until, finally, the child was gone. She had succumbed to the disease of adulthood."

I was curious as to what she meant by that, but reluctant to interrupt her, recognizing how precious this chance was to share her deepest memories. She took a sip of wine and continued.

"I wonder if the transition from child to adult must always kill what is fresh and genuine? Perhaps memories of those years of innocent joy are the tools we use to keep us strong and stable, while we enter the grown-up world of pain, embarrassment, or shyness."

Mom sat up a little straighter and looked me in the eye, her gentle smile changing into a sterner expression. I began to feel anxious, almost fearful of what I was about to hear. I knew her early life had been one of need and hardship.

"That little girl is sitting on steps attached to one of the most dilapidated, dirty, run-down houses in the entire town. Inside that house is a crippled, husbandless, frail woman who keeps six children alive from welfare check to welfare check. Her oldest sister is hidden away at a home for unwed mothers, waiting to bear the child conceived by one of the neighbors raping her. Behind the rickety, unpainted, wooden house runs a muddy, smelly river on whose banks you are likely to find anything from a used condom to a king-sized rat, or even a floating body. She is playing in the dirt because that is her small front yard; there is no lawn. She is barefoot because she has no shoes; shoes are a luxury of winter. She is wearing a torn, not-too-clean dress that, a few years before, had belonged to some other girl. When she looks into a mirror, she tries to keep her mouth closed, because even at age eight, her teeth are yellowing and decayed. In her school photographs, she learned to always cover her sweet smile with her hand. The dog is a stray mongrel who exists on neighborhood scraps. The hill she can see is much the same, but at the top, overlooking the river and field from a distance, are the respectable houses of the more fortunate. They feel bad about all that dirt and poverty down below, but have become conditioned to look past them toward the horizon. Her schoolmates, who have proper homes, don't seem to mind the girl's poverty, at least outwardly. She's an outgoing, bright and pretty child, oblivious to her situation. Realization will come later, and with it, shame and embarrassment. But the miracle is that this child did experience exuberance, joy and freedom."

I tried to picture the contrasting images Mom was painting with her words but I knew I could never put myself in the world of her childhood, with the smells, the sounds, and the feeling of being unprotected. I moved my chair closer, wanting her to know that I felt her pain, but also understood how, in spite of it all, she cherished the only childhood she had. I was taken by the astounding ability of a child to adapt to her surroundings, no matter how negative.

"Mom, I've never known you to be bitter or resentful, or even ashamed of your childhood. You always seemed so full of inner happiness. Where did your strength come from?"

"Strength comes from the joyful moments you treasure and hold in your heart."

I thought of the transition from child to adult. As self-awareness grows, we must compete; we must "play the game." There is no going back—the cumbersome yoke of responsibility blocks the way. New growth in the springtime is too far away on the ground. We don't see it, but only recall the memory of it: the smells, the blades of grass. We are too tired or busy to inspect each one, or catch crickets, or pull the blossoms off the weeds. We are touched by unseen forces, which have killed the child to nurture the adult.

Mom got up and took my arm. "Will you drive me somewhere? I want to show you something."

In my car, we headed south, towards the river and the center of town. She became more anxious. "Turn down this road. Right under the bridge."

We drove along a road parallel to the river lined with a few old houses, but mostly vacant lots and some new buildings. A sign read Peaceful Valley. The neighborhood looked as if it was becoming trendy, as nicer houses were being built.

"That's where our old shanty house was, right there, but now there's nothing. And there's the hill I climbed. Oh, and there's where Violet lived, and the old Basque who taught me how to count in Spanish."

We stopped the car and she got out. "Take a picture of me in front of the sign."

As I was focusing the camera, she smiled and stood proudly upright with her arm around the sign. "I want a picture of where the *good old days* were."

* * *

Mom is gone now. I live far from where she grew up. From time to time, I visit our hometown. For some reason, when I do, I always end up in Peaceful Valley. I like to think of the little girl named Ramona, who loved life, never seeing the squalor around her, and who ran, full of joy, through the mud and the sunlit spring grass.

From Spokane, Washington, Christine Bostrom studied History at the University of Washington, and has a degree in Spanish Philology from Western Washington University. At twenty, she began traveling in Europe and North Africa, and has traveled continuously since. Settled in Madrid since 1976, she now spends her time between Blaine, Washington, and Spain.

'Tis the Season

Barbara Clarke

This Christmas is not shaping up to be a good one. My father comes home at three in the morning after a boys-only poker party with his real estate pals. Dad sounds a little too jolly out in the hall talking to Mom and his "ho, ho, ho" doesn't sit well either. I fall back to sleep to the sound of their argument.

The next morning, Dad heads for work early and waves good-bye from the front door, leaving the inside air so filled with tension I long to play outside even if it's below freezing in St. Louis. Mom is barely speaking to anyone the whole day.

Just as we are finishing dinner, Mom looks daggers at Dad and says, "Christmas is on your father!" She finishes the dishes, leaves the kitchen, and a few minutes later shuffles into the living room in her bathrobe and slippers, carrying a pillow and a blanket. She makes her bed on the couch and turns her back to us.

I don't see why my brother, Bud, and I are being punished because of Dad, or that she has the right to cancel our Christmas. Dad, Bud, and I stand frozen in the living room like minor figures in a crèche wondering what to do. Since Dad looks clueless, Bud jerks me by my arm and leads me into the hall where we powwow in private.

"So much depends on us getting Dad to do Christmas this year," says Bud, who's twelve and taking the lead since I'm only seven and starting to cry. "Come on," he says and jerks me by the arm again, down the hall, and back into the living room.

"We want a damn tree," Bud says, his hands on his hips, keeping his back to Mom.

"Yeah," I chime in. Take charge, Dad, show her for once, I think, but am smart enough to let Bud's "damn" do the job.

Dad runs his hand over his balding head the way he does when he's thinking, which I take as a good sign. After what seems like forever, he gestures for me and Bud to join him in the hall.

"Christmas it is, kids," he says, with a smile—our hero—as we follow him into the hall. He's going to be jolly about our situation if it kills him. He reaches up, pulls on the cord to lower the attic ladder, and ascends.

Bud and I can hear him carefully stepping around overhead, looking for the boxes marked Xmas. Because the attic is unfinished, he has to navigate the wide planks to keep from falling through the ceiling. We stand at the foot of the stairs, looking into the dark void of the attic like stargazers.

Finally, Dad comes down with the boxes of lights and ornaments in his arms and hands them off to Bud. He reaches back, comes down with the tree stand, and then closes the attic ladder.

"Get your coats, kids. Let's go." We ignore Mom. I'm the last one out and let the front door stand open so that the cold air sweeps into the warm living room. She can get up and close it herself.

We go to the Boy Scout lot, buy a tree without the usual quarrel over the best one, rope it to the top of the car, drive home, and bring it in through the front door. More door standing open!

Dad and Bud settle the tree in the stand and string the lights while I assume Mom's role of ornament unwrapper and hand them off one at a time since we have certain places where they go. While Dad and Bud finish hanging the ornaments at the top, I make hot chocolate with extra marshmallows for the three of us. We sip our drinks and we ooh and aah over the way the tree has come together. We pretend to be having a great time while my mother, lying with her back to us, alternates between sighing and sniffling.

Bud and I toss on the tinsel, trying to be extra gay about the grim start to the holiday, until it's our bedtime. Dad stays up late neatly collecting our silver snarls and drapes the tinsel, strand by strand.

The next morning, we have our mother back. She leaves the couch and makes our breakfast as though nothing has happened. Like she's used my No. 2 pencil's rubber end. Erase. Erase.

Much like Bud's train set that we assemble under the tree, we mostly chug along with stops and starts to complete the tasks at hand. I help Mom get the house ready for Grandma Rosie and Grandpa John's visit on Christmas Day, and Dad doesn't go to any more parties.

This is how we do it—like the weatherman on the radio—storm approaching, it could be a big one, and then it passes.

* * *

The next Christmas, my mother oversees the neighborhood caroling group. We collect for a charity and sing our hearts out for several hours in the snow and cold.

This year Bud is chosen to go up, ring the doorbell, and ask for a donation for needy families. While we hum "O Little Town of Bethlehem," he blurts out "trick or treat" by mistake. The man standing in his doorway looks at my brother and laughs. While I feel bad for Bud, I will remind him of this for the next several Christmases.

Afterward everyone comes back to our house for mulled cider and cookies. As I move through the carolers jammed into our living room, passing cookies on a tray, I can smell the frost still clinging to their coats.

Our neighbor Lee, who is the handsomest man I've ever seen in real life, carols with us and joins my father out in the kitchen. Dad gets out the whiskey, and after a few drinks Lee comes back into the living room, finds me and Mom, and hugs us to him. In a deep voice, he sings *I saw Mommy kissing Santa Claus* and gives us both a kiss on the cheek. Mom blushes and I practically die from the touch of his lips on my face.

* * *

The following Christmas I'm out shopping with Mom. We're at the jewelry store looking for a present for my Uncle John and his new wife when I notice her pause at the case of wedding rings all shiny and golden.

"Wouldn't you like a new one, Mom?" She has a worn-out silver sliver of a wedding ring that reminds me of the metal band on the leg of the fresh turkey Mom and Grandma Rosie bought at the Soulard market for Thanksgiving.

"Mine's fine," she says, twisting it around her finger. "It's not that important. I'm not keeping up with the Joneses." I know she's thinking of the mothers' club ladies who come in fur coats to meetings and have twinkling diamond rings. I'm not convinced, since she pauses again at the ring case before we leave the store.

When I tell Dad about this, he agrees that her ring is old and worn. It doesn't take much of my nine-year-old charm and sincerity before we are off to the store three days before Christmas.

"She wants a band," I say, "wide and gold."

"Your daughter's right," the salesgirl behind the counter says. "That's what the ladies wear these days." We look at several, and then Dad points to the one I like.

"That one?" he asks, looking at me for my approval.

"Perfect," I say.

"Yes, a very good choice." The salesgirl gives Dad an approving smile. Now Dad's smiling and even springs for a velvet box and fancy gift wrap.

This year we are a real family and the four of us go to pick out the tree. Bud and I have our traditional squabble over the best one, take it home, put it on our back porch, and get back in the car. We drive through the Forest Park neighborhood where the rich people live, to see how they've decorated their houses, and end up walking around downtown to look at the department store window holiday displays.

"What do you think, Em?" Dad says to my mother after we've piled back into the cold car. "Shall we warm up at the Parkmoor, stay up late, and send these two off to bed with visions of sugar plums dancing in their heads? Waiting up for Santa?"

Bud groans and I snicker at the idea of Santa getting trotted out as the guy who brings the gifts. I can barely wait, though, until Mom opens her present the day after tomorrow.

We're not the only people who think the Parkmoor is a good idea, and have to wait for a table. Finally, we're seated and have a feast of onion rings and burgers, and pass one of their giant hot-fudge sundaes around the table. On the drive home, I have a variation of what Dad said—visions of holiday happiness dancing in my head.

On Christmas morning Mom looks so surprised when I hand her the little box from under the tree. It's the last gift to be opened.

"It's from Dad to you," I say, waiting for Dad to say something, but he just looks pleased and even a little shy.

"Oh, Dorsey," Mom says. Her voice twinkles like the glitter on the paper when she opens the box and sees the ring.

"Put it on her finger, Dad," I say, unable to control myself and what I think this occasion should look like. Sometimes Dad calls me "the little director." He gets up out of his chair, slips it on Mom's finger, and steps back. I say *until death do us part* to myself and hope they remember too.

"It's just beautiful," Mom says, looking up at Dad and then over at me. "Thank you. Both of you." When my mother gets up to show her mother the ring, I take her by the arm and stand her under the mistletoe in the doorway to the dining room.

"Dad," I say, nodding toward Mom. Now *she* looks a little shy. They quickly kiss on the lips and both blush while I clap.

Barbara Clarke's memoir, Getting to Home: Sojourn in a Perfect House, *was published in 2009.* "Good Vibrations" *appeared in the online magazine* Full Grown People *in 2015. Named "best body" in ninth grade and more recently "most likely to start a forgiveness movement," Barbara is the happiest when you call her "an author."*

One Word, Two Little Letters

Lisa Dailey

I dropped into an easy chair and snapped open my laptop, ready to reconnect with the world, finally checked into a hotel that offered wi-fi. While my husband and two teenage sons raced to find the pool, I stayed behind excited to catch up on news from friends and family back in the U.S. We were three months into a trip around the world and had been without wi-fi, and thus out of contact, for several days. For three months our only means of communication had been through e-mail, which made every word that came through precious. In reading those few simple lines of text, feelings of homesickness and travel weariness were washed away and my whole spirit lifted.

I drummed my fingers on the laptop, impatient as my browser connected and new messages were retrieved. Thrilled to see an e-mail from my cousin, I happily opened it first. But my elation turned to concern as she filled me in about an encounter with my one-time best friend, Hannah. My cousin explained that Hannah had been diagnosed with breast cancer and was undergoing chemotherapy. She described Hannah as looking quite ill with no hair and pasty skin—the epitome of cancer patient post chemo. With a troubled heart, I flashed through my relationship with Hannah and meditated on whether I should reach out to her.

I first met this slight, boyish, spitfire of a girl named Hannah in second grade. Although the smallest in her class until well into high school, Hannah's demeanor was exactly the opposite. Her no-nonsense, in-your-face, tell-it-like-it-is attitude instantly piqued my interest. Her incredible energy and spark of sassiness drew me to her. Her personality shone brightest in our dull, small town of Butte, Montana. I knew without a doubt that Hannah and I would become fast friends. We lived in the same apartment complex, went to school together, spent each weekend together, got into trouble, and did all the things best friends do growing up. We even called each other's mom "Mom." We were sisters. We were inseparable.

Our unity continued into high school, but boys and sports and different class schedules took their toll on the friendship, and Hannah and I drifted somewhat. Looking back, I believe jealousy contributed to our separation. I was developing into a young woman with bright blue eyes and curves in all the right places. Hannah was the "late bloomer" and still the immature tomboy who hadn't even started her period. I was popular and she wasn't, and I let it go to my head.

After high school, Hannah and I reconnected when we found ourselves in many of the same classes at the local college. As if there had been no discontinuity at all, we picked right back up where we had left off and resumed our regular routine of talking and hanging out. We had both matured—Hannah had blossomed into a young woman and I had stopped reading my worth in what everyone else thought of me. Thrilled to have her by my side again, our friendship sailed along smoothly until I decided I'd had enough of small-town living. I quit college, said goodbye to Hannah, and moved to Bellingham, Washington.

Despite the distance, our bond endured. Hannah and I often held marathon phone conversations and I would spend as much time as possible with her on my visits to Butte. As I navigated my way through the trials and tribulations of a new city, apartment, and job, I knew I could count on Hannah to cheer me on, give advice, or lend me a shoulder to cry on. When I fell in love, I realized my boyfriend, Ray, would have to pass the Hannah test. Thankfully, he won her over and in short order, Ray and I were saying "I do" with Hannah standing by our side as maid of honor. It didn't take long before Ray and I decided to expand our family.

When I gave birth to my first son, Hannah visited within days. Motherhood did not resemble anything I anticipated. There was no instant falling in love with my child, there was no glow of motherhood. I was wrecked. I had a debilitating bout of postpartum adjustment disorder. While not full-blown clinical depression, this temporary bout of the "Baby Blues" hindered regular sleeping and eating, thus exacerbating my depression. For a week Hannah made me dinner, forced me to eat and sleep, watched the baby, and helped nurse me back to a place of relative normalcy.

Eighteen months later I welcomed a second son and Hannah was by my side again. During this visit, Hannah asked if I would be a bridesmaid in her upcoming wedding. In short order, I stood by her side as Hannah married the love of her life and within a few short months, Hannah was expecting her first child.

For months, Hannah and I planned and planned my visit to Montana when she delivered. I would help her through those first trying days, just as she had done for me. I saved essential items I knew would help ease her transition into motherhood, I collected special outfits my children had outgrown, and I saved books on motherhood and parenting that had helped me along the way. I prepared to leave within a day of her call. My excitement for Hannah could barely be contained.

And then the day arrived. Hannah phoned and said labor had begun and she would call when the baby arrived. But I didn't hear from her that day. Or the next. I called and called and called the hospital trying to talk to her, but her line only repeated a busy signal. Why hadn't she called me? Was something wrong? Had something bad happened to the baby? Or to Hannah? My mind churned with thoughts of every conceivable tragedy. I finally told the nurse that I was Hannah's best friend calling from two states away and beside myself with concern. The nurse explained in HIPAA-compliant, vague language that the birth had been quite rough at times, but mom and baby girl continued to rest quietly in between a stream of visitors. Much relieved, I waited for Hannah's call.

When Hannah and I finally connected, the first question I asked was not, "How are you?" or "How is the baby?" I didn't wait for Hannah to offer details. I knew she and baby girl were in satisfactory condition. The nurse had assured me of that, but she also had said things were "quite rough." The first words out of my mouth were, "Did you have a C-section?" Immediately, Hannah became reserved. Distant. We spoke a bit more, but her tone was flat, her answers abrupt. I wrote it off as exhaustion and waited for more news.

Hannah phoned a few days later and through tears and shaky voice told me how badly I had upset her. She didn't want me to come to Montana and, in fact, didn't want to see me ever again. She felt she had lingered in my shadow her whole life and with my five little words, one question, she believed I was asserting my motherhood superiority and looking for a way to shove her right back in the shadows by judging anything other than a natural birth to somehow be inferior. With those five little words, everything changed. I had broken our friendship.

Hannah's call caught me completely off guard and shattered my heart. Devastated, I sobbed for days scrambling to find a way to restore the friendship. I called Hannah's mom pleading for advice, but she said I needed to give Hannah time to cool off and things would eventually return to normal. I wrote Hannah letters apologizing for making her so angry and hurting her so badly. I wrote that it was never my intention to upset her in any way. My thoughts centered around her well-being. I mailed the effects I had collected for her, wishing she'd feel the love in my heart.

I grieved over the loss of this friendship for years. When I lost Hannah, I closed myself off and had difficulty making new friends. I built a wall around my heart and kept myself to myself. Losing Hannah cost me my best friend as well as potential new friends. It took years for me to trust myself enough to let my guard down and open my heart to others. Having the power to destroy a long-term friendship in seconds, I remained cautious for fear of hurting others with careless words.

For years I tried to win back Hannah's friendship. I continued to send Christmas cards and call when I returned to Butte. Eventually, Hannah relented and allowed me to meet her daughter, then almost three years old. I saw Hannah several more times through the years when I returned home for visits and again at our high-school reunion. But there were no more two-hour phone conversations. There were no more birthday cards or thinking-of-you notes. There were no more spontaneous trips to Spokane, halfway between Butte and Bellingham, just to spend time with each other for the weekend. The natural ebb and flow of a relationship ceased to exist.

Ten years after our friendship fell apart, I lost my mom to cancer. Per Mom's wishes, I was to phone each of her contacts, including Hannah, to let them know she was gone. I wandered aimlessly through the hospice garden searching for the words to tell Hannah that the woman she too had called "Mom" had passed. I anticipated her sadness and thought she would be sympathetic to my grief. I imagined all those years of frigidity melting away and this shared loss being the spark that rekindled our friendship. In the calm of the garden, with shaking hands and heart in my throat, I tentatively dialed Hannah's number. She answered and I explained I was calling to let her know my mom had lost her battle with cancer and died. After a brief pause, she responded in one word.

"Oh."

Not, "I'm so sorry for your loss."

Not, "I'm sorry to hear that."

Not even, "That's too bad."

Just, "Oh."

And then silence.

So much feeling was conveyed in one word, just two little letters. I heard all the hurt and jealousy and iciness still lingering in her heart. With that one-word response, I knew nothing could ever repair this friendship. I had to stop wishing for it to be better. There would never be a reconciliation.

And with that realization, I stopped. I stopped calling, I stopped sending Christmas cards, and I stopped visiting when I was in Butte. I erased her contact information from my phone, her address from my address book, and her hold on my heart.

I will forever feel bad that my few words wounded Hannah so deeply. I will forever feel sorry that she interpreted my question as a judgment instead of hearing the love and concern in my heart. I will forever feel sad that she couldn't express her anger to me, hear my apology, and continue our friendship. I hope she doesn't carry that hurt and anger all these years later.

So much can depend upon so little . . . a handful of words can lift your spirits or gravely wound a friendship, and just the smallest of words—just two little letters—can destroy it forever.

Sitting at my laptop half a world away, sad to hear she was ill, I knew that inaction was the best choice. Reaching out to her would have been a mistake. "Hey, I'm on a trip of a lifetime, traveling the world with my family, sorry to hear you have cancer." Instead, I closed my eyes and sent only mental thoughts of healing and love. Content with my chosen path, I moved on to my next e-mail in search of words to lift my spirit.

Lisa Dailey is an avid traveler and writer. She is currently working on her memoir, Square Up, detailing the adventures and misadventures of a seven-month trip around the world, as well as her own personal journey through overwhelming grief. You can read more about Lisa's adventures on her blog NorthwestRambles.com

The Word for No Words

Victoria Doerper

Dad and I fidgeted through the day in our own isolated
little worlds. I paced in front of the window. Below me
people hurried across the street oblivious to the hospital's shadow looming over them. Dad read a newspaper.
We took the elevator down to the hospital cafeteria.
Brushed crumbs off a round table, sat down on blue
plastic chairs, picked at our plates without noticing
what we ate. We escaped the nauseating antiseptic air
by walking outside into the familiar and comforting
scent of car exhaust. Returning to the operating room
waiting area, Dad read a magazine. I sat, gazing down,
noticed a thread dangling from the uneven hem of my
blouse. One straggly beige thread. What if I pulled it?
Would I tidy up the ragged edge or would the whole
fabric start to unravel? Double doors whooshed open
and Mom's surgeon emerged. His green surgical mask
hung down around his neck. He looked like a clean-
shaven Chinese sage. I searched his weary face for a
sign.

* * *

Mom had always warmed our world with conversation
and social interaction. She arranged celebrations for

special occasions and she hosted dinners, barbecues, and pool parties for no special reason at all. In any group of people, I could always spot my tall, red-haired, blue-eyed mother, her gentle features animated with interest in an old friend or a new acquaintance. I marveled at how she managed to remember the large and small details of people's lives. She'd check in about the father who'd had an operation, or the brother who'd gotten a new job a few months before, or she'd query a neighbor about something simple, like how that new crockpot purchased a few weeks ago was working out. Ever attentive to her family, she shopped, cooked, cleaned, took my brother to school events. She welcomed Dad home after work with a cocktail, dinner, and conversation about the day. Mom was social director, homemaker, cheerleader, chief comforter. She wasn't an incessant talker, but she was never at a loss for words. My dad and I, indisputable introverts, floated quietly on the waves of her easy conversation and kindness.

Mom was fifty-four years old when she had the heart attack. One evening in the spring of 1973, she felt a strange sensation in her throat, a cool fullness as if she'd just swallowed a peppermint. She thought it would go away. After all, this was not crushing chest pain. Besides, she had a clean bill of health from a recent annual checkup. So she delayed going to the doctor until after the birthday party she'd planned for my dad, just a few days away. While she delayed, part of her heart tissue was dying.

The doctor at the local community hospital thought the heart attack was mild. But after a series of tests he discovered damage to the heart muscle as well as occluded arteries. Mom needed a heart bypass. The complex procedure, not a routine surgery in the early seventies, sounded frightening, but with no reasonable alternative, Mom was scheduled for surgery in a few weeks at Saint Vincent's hospital, forty minutes from home, where experienced surgeons staffed a heart specialty unit.

I was twenty-four years old, living four hundred miles away. Dad still worked full time. My brother, fourteen, was barely in high school. We all needed the strong, capable woman who was Mom. Our anchor. We needed the gregarious, energetic, fun-loving, kind, and comforting social center of our small family.

* * *

The heart surgery failed. Excision of so much damaged heart tissue (significant damage, the surgeon had said) caused the remaining tissue to strain away from the sutures with each heartbeat. Within two days the sutured-together tissue tore open. Mom underwent two more surgeries during that fifteen-day hospital stay, one so urgent it was performed while she lay on the bed in her room. That final surgery deprived her brain of oxygen for a time and caused a stroke. She stayed in ICU for days, then finally stabilized.

I didn't want to leave, but I had to get back to my job in northern California. I whispered pleading prayers every day for Mom to heal, and I stayed in touch with daily phone calls to my dad, first with hospital updates, then with news from the rehab center where Mom was recuperating.

"How's Mom?" I asked one evening. "Shouldn't she be going home soon?"

"She's doing better, but they need to do a little more therapy."

"What kind of therapy?"

"She can't use her right hand very well. She has a problem with her speech, too. I forget what the doctor called it."

"You mean . . . paralysis?" I could barely choke out the word.

"No, it's not that. I mean the word for having no words. Asia or something."

I flew home a few days before Mom was scheduled for discharge from the rehab center. Lying on a hospital bed in her small room at the center, she looked so fragile. Her chest had been slashed open three times for the surgeries; a long wound on her thigh mapped where vessels had been removed for the heart bypass graft. Her graceful, slender hands and arms were smudged blue-black where multiple IV needles had been stabbed.

Dad and I kissed her, said words of which I have no recollection. Mom, still alert and intelligent, clearly had something to say to us. But she could not find the words. Frustration clouded her eyes. That's when I learned the doctor's word for no words. Aphasia. An ugly, hateful word. A monstrous word. A cold clinical word that meant damage to regions of the brain associated with language, a heartless condition that locked people inside themselves, rendering them unable to speak what they longed to say. Mom struggled to make her thoughts known, but all that came out were sounds, more like moans or grunts. Surely there must be another way. When a nurse with a clipboard walked into the room, I asked to borrow pen and paper so we could exchange notes with Mom.

"Oh, no, honey," the nurse responded, "That won't help."

I must have looked shocked, because she went on to explain that Mom couldn't read or write. "She'll regain some of her abilities, but probably not all of them. Time will tell."

A couple of days later, Mom came home. All of us were numb and uncertain, finding our way in a new territory, and Mom most of all. Weak and often in pain, she could only move slowly from room to room, sit or lie on the couch, watch the rest of us make a hash of tasks she did expertly without even thinking about them. She couldn't answer questions about what needed to be done. Worse than that, my sociable, independent mother couldn't use the telephone though it rang frequently with friends calling to check in.

One late afternoon not quite a week after Mom returned home, the discharge coordinator from the rehab center called. Would Mom be willing to visit Pat, a woman who had been in rehab with her? Pat lived alone and needed some company. Dad relayed the question to Mom. Even though Mom gained strength each day, I thought such a visit would be too much too soon. But Mom immediately nodded her assent.

The next day, with some trepidation, I drove Mom to Pat's nearby apartment. When we arrived, I bungled a simple parking maneuver, causing Mom to wince with each jarring bump against the curb. Mortified, I hopped out and opened the passenger door, trying not to jolt her as I helped her struggle to her feet. I suggested she use the wheelchair I'd brought, but she refused. She accepted my arm, though, and we toddled in halting steps up the cement walkway to the front door. I knocked, and after a minute or two, a thickset woman with short salt-and-pepper hair greeted us. She smiled; Mom smiled. We went inside.

Morning sun streamed in the windows of the tiny apartment. Sunny yellow. The kitchen curtains were white with strawberry red flowers. On the side table, a smooth gray ceramic elephant raised its trunk in salute. The fragrance of fresh-brewed coffee imbued the room with comfort. At first we just stood in the living room, frozen in a moment charged with uncertainty, silent and still. What should I do, I wondered. I should be able to do something helpful. Then the tableau animated when Pat's gravelly voice made a primitive noise.

"Ahhht!" she said, expelling the abrupt sound with some effort. She walked to the kitchen and pointed at the coffee pot.

Mom looked over at Pat.

"Uhhht!" Mom managed to press out.

I couldn't manage anything but a nod. Mom and I sat down on the sofa. Pat poured coffee into thick white mugs and brought them to the coffee table.

Finally Pat settled herself into a tired recliner on the other side of the small living room. She leaned forward, took a sip of coffee. "Ahhht!" she repeated, but it didn't mean what it had before. She wasn't looking at the coffee pot. She was looking at Mom. What could she possibly mean?

Pause.

"Uhhhch!" Mom responded.

Pause.

"Ockhh!" Pat barked.

Pause.

"Auhh!" Mom breathed.

Guttural sounds with no discernible meaning bounced like a basketball between them. I remembered when I was a child sounding out the letters of the alphabet. Alone the sounds were nonsense, but when I stitched them together they could make words with rich, varied, and precise meanings. I loved words and language. And what I heard between Mom and Pat was not that. I felt a bubble of hysteria rising in my chest. This exchange was absurd. Heartbreaking. Cruel. This monstrous aphasia.

I wanted to run back out into the normal world and take Mom with me as herself again. But I sat, not moving, feeling sick to my stomach, a powerless bystander witnessing a strained, unmapped struggle to engage in some sort of conversation. I had words in my brain, so many wonderful words, and I sat there, with my health and my physical capability, unable to utter one of them. But Mom and Pat, whose strokes had unraveled their sophisticated language of words, gave each other the only sounds they had left. Broken, wounded sounds. Individually, the sounds meant nothing. But as Mom and Pat wove their ragged vocal exhalations together, the meaning became profound. It wasn't conversation exactly. A more precise word for it would have been communion.

In about half an hour, the visit ended. Mom and Pat embraced. Mom took my arm and we made our slow way back to the car. I held the door as she leaned against the frame and sank down into the seat. She looked exhausted. Had this been too much for her? It had almost been too much for me. I slid into the driver's seat, relieved to be in a place where things worked as they were supposed to. When I put the key in the ignition the engine would spring to life; when I slipped the gear lever into drive and pressed on the gas pedal, the car would move. I leaned on the console and turned to look at Mom, who had slumped forward a bit.

"Are you doing okay?" I asked.

She nodded her head slowly. Then, straightening up slightly, she gave me a weak smile, reached over, patted my hand. *She* was comforting *me*. I cast my eyes down. Why couldn't I be more like Mom instead of my socially awkward, ineffective self? Then I noticed our hands, hers still resting on top of mine. How alike they were. I had Mom's hands. The slender fingers, slightly ridged nails, thin wrists. Maybe, some day, I would have her strength and grace too. I turned the key, put the car in gear, stepped on the gas. We moved forward.

Victoria Doerper writes memoir, poetry, and non-fiction. Her poetry appears in Sue C. Boynton 2013 Winning Poem Chapbook , Noisy Water Poetry Anthology, Clover, A Literary Rag, Cirque, and These Fragile Lilacs. Her prose appears in Orion Magazine and the Red Wheelbarrow Writers anthology, Memory into Memoir.

In Hindsight

Emily Duryee

If you want to be a happy and successful writer, so much depends upon getting an "A" in tenth-grade English class. This was my "A" paper . . . if only . . .

Assignment: Write a five-paragraph essay describing your New Year's resolution. In the introduction include a thesis that specifically states your resolution and why it is important to you. In the body include an example in each of the three paragraphs of how you will fulfill your resolution. The conclusion will summarize and demonstrate your ability to succeed.

Liberty Rose Prescott
Mr. Higsby's 10th Grade English Class
Room 304
Morning Block
Draft 1

How I Won't Achieve My New Year's Resolution!
Paragraph One: Introduction and Thesis

Over two and a half years ago, after my twin sister Destiny Amber Prescott, Little Miss Sunastic, Washington's Ultimate Grand Supreme Beauty Queen, took the dirt nap, gave up the dust, communed with tumbleweeds, hit the dimmer switch, snuffled the candle out, patty-caked with the grim reaper, belly-flopped into heaven; Geez, Mr. Higsby, must I spell it out for you: she croaked, as in died, while I, Liberty Rose Prescott, fifth runner-up in Sunastic, Washington's Fourth of July pie-eating contest, survived and single-handedly destroyed Darwin's theory of the "survival of the fittest." Oh, and when I say Destiny died, I mean it as a metaphor for the complete disintegration of my relationship with my father. Death, sounds more dramatical, don't you think?!

Paragraph Two: Definition

"Metaphor: A figure of speech in which a term is transferred from the object it ordinarily designates to an object it may designate only by implicit comparison or analogy." Hmm, that doesn't make a lick of sense to me, but anyhoo . . .

Paragraph Three: Continue to Drive Introduction and Thesis Home

I made . . . made . . . made the same resolution three years running: It's up to me to save my screwed-up family. It's very, very, very important to me. *Why* is so obvious, typed in Times New Roman 12-point font, so therefore, in the following paragraphs (please don't count how many) I will detail how I was and still remain unable to fulfill this resolution.

Paragraph Four: I guess this is what you'd refer to as the body of my paper, because it's so meaty.

Philip Ryan Prescott. Bailed. On New Year's Eve! Left our family high and dry. After a minor domestic dispute in which my "bitchy-nagging-selfish mom" accused my "stupid-angry-asshole dad" of cheating with his office assistant Deidra. Sidebar: Mr. Higsby, before you go

putting child protective services on speed dial, here's a
quick replay of their minor domestic dispute.

Start of Scene

On New Year's Eve around 7:03 pm, my parents
quarantined themselves off in their bedroom for world
war scream number 962. They're probably pacing each
other like two caged tigers; pacing . . . eyes locked . . .
pacing . . . hearts thudding . . . pacing . . . ragged breaths
. . . pacing . . . anger festering . . . pacing . . . guilt simmering . . . simmering fire-roasted marshmallows . . .
those sound good . . . I'm starving . . . seriously you can
hear my stomach growling . . . pacing . . . until . . .

Dad pounced first. "If you're so unhappy, then why
don't you divorce me?"

"Maybe I should!" Mom yelled.

From deep in my self-improvement lair (the lumpy
living room couch blanketed by self-helpers) my inter-
nal alarm went off. "Parental-discord alert: WHOO!
OOOH! Parental-discord alert: WHOO! OOOH!" I
jumped up from the couch lightning-fast (okay, quick
enough to give me a head rush) so of course my self-
helper, *Cussing with Class* by James Footenmouth, goes
a-flying.

"This is not a drill!" I crackled to the floor like a bag
of potato chips. "I repeat this is not a drill," I whisper-
yelled into the wooden floorboards (not descriptive
enough) muddled-gray shag. I military-crawled across
the living room shag (a million miles) all the while,
wondering when was the last time I vacuumed? I still
couldn't pinpoint the exact date of said chore, when my
bruised knees, I mean, rug-burned knees hit kitchen tile.

"Chores can wait. The mission comes first." I
sneezed; scratch that, spit carpet lint from my teeth. I

back-flipped (too much) I somersaulted to my feet or I would have, if I weren't so breathless and klutzy. From the cabinet, I removed a glass tumbler and hit the deck (but more gingerly this time; I didn't need to bleed out from broken glass.) Using the speed and agility of a banana slug, I slithered down the hallway past my brother's room (which was pretty tricky with a listening glass in my right hand). As per usual, my brother Nick was mindlessly throwing grenades at virtual monsters; our parents' screams deafened by videogame *booms, blasts, kabooms,* and *splats.*

Huffin' outside my parents' bedroom, I held the tumbler to my ear and leaned against the door, which was pretty pointless because A) They were screaming; make that, auditioning for a horror flick. B) I was losing my grip on the glass. So, long story short, I'm trembling like a dachshund after she tunneled her way through a snow drift except it's almost January in Sunastic so we've still got the A/C cranked up. Speaking of wiener dogs, (the books say puppies are warm furballs of unconditional love and therefore ideal candidates for helping humans overcome grief; but of course we're not allowed to own a furry wiener 'cuz of Mom's allergies).

So anyhoo, there I was shaking like a hypothermic dachshund without my lil' knitted sweater, and Dad yelled, "Then do it. Damn it!"

"Gladly!" screamed Mom. "Let me help you pack. Let's start with the Christmas present you gave me!"

CRASH! What was that? It sounded like glass shattering, which was odd because my glass tumbler was still affixed to my ear.

"Are you crazy? That vase was Waterford, b****," Dad said.

"Parental-violence alert: WHOO! OOOH!" I set the tumbler on the shag and ran for the broom and dust pan. "Parental-violence alert: WHOO! OOOH!" I rushed back to their room and yanked open their door in three seconds flat (true story).

"Whoa, everyone calm down, okay?" I swung the broom in front of me as if waving a white flag.

"Why don't you take your broken vase to Deidra, you ass—"

"Ho-o-o-ld on . . . Remember, I read in *Shut Up Before You Make Someone Throw Up: Ten Proven Techniques of Nonviolent Communication* by Dr. Yanni Asschbachwerd that—" Mom and Dad froze, clearly enraptured . . . okay, they were stunned into silence, but I'd take it. "—we should take a deep breath and think before we say words that can never be taken back. In through our nose, out through our open mouths . . . Huuuh," I inhaled. "Haaaaaaaath," I exhaled.

"Shut up!" Mom and Dad said in unison.

"Okay, that was a classic example of Dumpster Dialoging—" But it was as if they had tunnel vision for each other. Or they were in a dark tunnel and their marriage was about to become road kill. I swear, Dad's warm brown eyes turned black and hollow. *He wouldn't hurt Mom? Boom-boom*, my heart thudded. *Us? Boom-boom. Himself? BOOM-BOOM. Would he? Boom-boom-boom-boom-Boom.*

I channeled my inner Wonder Woman and put my heart attack (too over the top), panic-attacking heart on ice. "This whole thing sounds like a big ole' misunderstanding." I ran my tongue over my braces just to see if I could bleed. Turns out I can. "Er, let's drop it." I clapped them to attention.

"I'm sooo done. Phill, I'm done."

"Nothing that can't be fixed," I blurted. "Who wants to use nonviolent speak? Anyone? Anyone?!" I tugged on Mom's blouse.

"Right back at you,*$@%#," Dad said.

It only took Dad two minutes and thirty-four seconds to pack all his earthly belongings into a carry-on suitcase.

"Tell Nick I'm sorry." He wheeled his black (too generic) titanium steel suitcase toward the front door. "I tried . . . I can't—"

"Dad, you don't have to do this. Just stay, okay? Let's work this out," I begged.

"You know how much I love you kids. But I have to go. I can't deal . . . I can't deal with . . . your mother."

"You can't leave." My arms swung out like a crossing guard. "We need you." I reached for his suitcase. "I need you."

"Move, Liberty, get out of my way!" He grabbed the suitcase and pushed me aside.

Thwack . . . my shoulder rammed the wall (told ya, I'm klutzy.)

Thwack . . . the door slammed behind him.

"Dad." I opened the front door. "Dad," I screamed at the back of his head. His shoulders sagging, he hefted the suitcase into the trunk and whammed it shut. His car door creaked when he opened it. An old man climbed inside.

"Dad," I hollered. He glanced out the rearview mirror. "Dad, don't go!" I bounded down the porch steps. "Dad, wait!" He hit the gas. "Come back," I said to the exhaust.

End of Scene

Paragraph Five (or however you want to count it): Conclusion

In conclusion, refer to the previous paragraphs which summarize my utter lack of ability to fix my screwed-up family. Obviously, this assignment proves, I have not succeeded. But I won't give up. It's up to me to fix my family.

* * *

The morning I got my graded paper back, my heart skidded and stumbled like a drunken frat boy making his way to the bar during last call. It said ungradable in red letters.

Miss Prescott, and I'm paraphrasing because I could barely make out his cursive, *your writing displays a flair for the dramatics better suited for a low-budget Lifetime movie than my College Predatory* (it was a P-word of some sort) *class that focuses on grammar and academic* (or was it epidemic) *writing. Your five-paragraph essay, if we can even call it an essay, shows that you are unable at this time to follow the simplest of rules and writing guidelines.*

In retrospect, he was probably right. Back then I didn't know a semicolon from a colon or if my colon needed a colonoscopy. While I didn't earn an "A" on the paper, he did share my essay with others; most notably the attendance counselor, and his rabbi or maybe his pet rabbit? Not to point fingers, but he needed a crash course in penmanship.

"I discussed 'your paper' at length with Principal Frost. We think it's best if we remove you, effective immediately, from this class and place you in a morning Free Think period in the library for 'creative thinkers.' " He ushered me to the door.

"Words are very powerful." I leaned in and whispered, "ve-ry po-wer-ful."

Emily Duryee dreamed of being a writer since the fourth grade when she won a scholarship to the Wenatchee Valley Writers conference for her story, "Monsters Under the Floorboards." She learns from writing workshops, great books, fellow writers and mentors: Betty Scott, Laura Kalpakian, Cami Ostman, Robert Dugoni, and Donald Maass.

The Foreman

Seán Dwyer

"Hon, we're off to Three-Forty," Dad said.

"Three-Forty, here we come!" I exclaimed. Mom stepped out of the kitchen, gave Dad a kiss, and ruffled my crew cut.

"Be good for Daddy," she told me. "Make sure Daddy and Uncle Tom build a nice bathroom for Grandpa."

I hugged her slim legs. "I will," I replied. "Uncle Tom said I'm going to be the foreman. That's important."

"Yes, it is," Mom said. She winked at Dad.

We piled into the blue Oldsmobile and drove to Three-Forty, our nickname for my grandparents' house at 340 Adams Street. They also owned "Monroe" and a couple of other houses Grandpa had bought in the mid-1920s.

I liked Three-Forty, but it wasn't so good for kids. It sat on a block crammed with tall, narrow houses. The front yards were useful for ten-yard dashes and little more. The backyards could serve as a mini-baseball field. I once spent a week visiting my grandparents. I made friends with the neighbor kids, but there wasn't much to do.

Now it was Grandpa's turn to visit us. Mom didn't want the noise we made while building his bathroom to bother him. In the evenings, Grandpa liked to sit on the couch and tell me stories about his days as a train engineer. I was happy he was visiting us instead of his other grandkids, because I was getting to know him better.

Three-Forty had only one toilet, on the second floor. You had to climb twelve oak stairs, turn left at a landing, and climb six more stairs to reach all of the bedrooms and the bathroom. The bathroom stood at the far end of the hallway, so my eighty-four-year-old Grandpa still faced a hike after climbing all those stairs.

Now the doctor said he had to stay off the stairs. Uncle Tom put a twin bed downstairs for him so he could sleep in the corner of the huge dining room. But he needed a bathroom, because he shouldn't have to use a bedpan for however many years he was going to live. It wasn't dignified, Mom said.

I didn't understand why the doctor said Grandpa couldn't go upstairs. Mom explained that he was tired after working fifty years and getting eight kids out the door into successful lives. I thought the stairs were easy. I could run up to the top without stopping. Coming down was more of a problem. My little sister missed a step once. I watched her roll sideways to the bottom, face-hair-face-hair, a look of surprise in her eyes. As soon as she popped up and smiled instead of crying, I laughed at the spectacle. Mom yelled at me for that.

The dining room at Three-Forty took up a quarter of the ground floor, so there was space for a half-bath in the corner closest to the kitchen plumbing. Uncle Tom, who worked in management for U.S. Steel in Gary, Indiana, was handy with tools. My aunt's husband, Uncle Paul, also worked for U.S. Steel, and he could help a lot too. The important guy, though, was Dad, who had built our house by himself and left U.S. Steel to work construction. Uncle Tom, Uncle Paul, and Dad had all the experience and tools they needed to do the work. But they still needed one more person: a foreman. They picked me. At age seven, I was on my way in the construction business.

It was summer and I had some playing to do, but I had to do my job first. We needed to get Grandpa's bathroom built fast. I thought I was a good choice for foreman because I knew the difference between a two-by-four and a one-by-eight, and I knew how to give orders. I used Dad's heavy, metal tape measure to check the width of the two-by-fours. When a board came up short, I called Dad over.

"This board isn't four inches wide, Dad," I said.

"That's just a name for the size of the board. They're always a bit less than two inches by four inches. It's okay." Even as a foreman, there were things I could learn.

It was Friday, and Dad had taken off work. We went into Grandpa's basement to plumb the new bathroom. I held the ladder for Dad because the concrete floor sloped toward a drain. The basement was dimly lit, and I also worried that he would miss a step on the way down. He cut a pipe in half and added a connector. Then he ran a long pipe from it under the dining room. I handed him the brackets he needed to secure the sink and toilet pipes, then he tapped holes in the floor to mark where to make his cuts for the toilet and the sink.

Dad gave me a lot of jobs to supervise. I checked for quality control when he cut the hole in the floor for the toilet. I held the front door open for him while he carried in the light fixture, the new white toilet, and the matching sink. I held the ladder while he nailed boards into the ceiling along the rafters. I helped him frame the new room, carrying studs to him and holding them while he sawed them to the exact length he needed. I reminded him to measure twice and cut once. I hugged the studs tightly at floor level while he hammered them into place at the ceiling. I also got to help him connect an electrical wire from the dining-room light to the wall above the location of the new sink.

On the weekend, my uncles came to help Dad and me. When they were there, they held the boards and helped pound the nails. All I had to do was supervise. The hands-off work was far less tiring than the manual labor, but I didn't mind pitching in when two-thirds of the crew was absent. That's the difference between an okay foreman and a great one.

At one point, I was sitting inside the bathroom space while Dad and my uncles sawed and hammered. Uncle Tom called me over to the other side of the dining room. He held a scrap of two-by-four and a 16d nail in his hands.

"Hey, Buddy, why don't you see if you can spell your name in the wood with nail holes?"

"I can do that!" I grabbed a hammer and a carpenter's pencil and set to work, glancing up once in a while to make sure the builders weren't running into trouble. I sketched my name with the pencil. It was hard to write with, because it was flat and broad so it wouldn't roll away. I tapped in the nail at intervals short enough to make the letters legible. A couple of times, I pounded the nail in far enough that I had to use the claw to yank it out, but I never smashed my thumb.

I showed my crew the board when I finished. Uncle Tom held it up and said, "Would you look at that! We should put it on the wall in the bathroom." Uncle Paul and Dad agreed, so Uncle Tom nailed the board to one of the studs on the outer wall, down low where I could see it.

With the studs up, Dad was able to wire the switch for the bathroom light. When the light came on, I clapped, and they joined in. The crew also got the water running that day. Hearing the toilet flush and watching the tap run and the sink drain made me really proud of what we had accomplished.

The next weekend, I held the front door while Dad and Uncle Tom carried sheets of drywall into the dining room. Uncle Paul asked me if I thought we needed insulation. I told him we didn't because the new walls didn't face outdoors. The crew agreed, and they nailed up the drywall in no time. I was sorry to see my name covered up, but I knew it would always be there. I held the tape for Dad, and I troweled on a bit of spackle down near the floor so Dad didn't have to bend over as far.

With the walls finished inside and out, the bathroom now offered enough privacy for Grandpa and Grandma to use it. Grandma had also been advised to avoid the stairs but had not yet been forbidden to use them, like Grandpa. But we weren't done with our work. We got the door framed and hung, then Dad painted the taped drywall a pale yellow to match the dining room. While he painted, I looked out the dining-room window at the backyard. The long grassy space between the back porch and the garage beckoned to me. Soon, I thought, I'd be done building and back to enjoying my summer, catching and releasing grasshoppers, teaching myself to pitch with a baseball-sized rubber ball, and climbing our four elms.

That evening, we took Grandpa home. I watched him shuffle to the bathroom and close the door. A bit later, I heard the toilet flush and the sink run, and he came out and went to bed. I hugged him and Grandma good-bye. Dad and I stepped into the summer twilight as an electric train rattled by on nearby tracks. The overhead wires created a trail of pink lightning that followed the engine and hung over the unsuspecting passengers.

When we got to our Oldsmobile, Dad used the wipers and washer fluid to remove a thin layer of rust-colored flue dust, brought down by the coming dew. The sky was still full of smoke from the steel mill, but the cool air cleared it every night. We drove home and told Mom the bathroom was finished. Dad said the work had gone faster and easier than he had expected.

Before I went to bed, Dad called me over to where he and Mom were sitting on the couch. Something jingled in his palm.

"Hold out your hand," he said.

I extended my arm, and he dropped four huge coins into my palm. They were so heavy I almost dropped them.

"Grandma wanted me to give these to you for helping so much."

"For being the foreman," I said.

I stared into my hand. I'd never seen coins like these, with the face of a woman who had long, flowing hair. They were the size of the Canadian silver dollar I'd bought with my saved allowance the year before.

"What are they?" I asked.

"They're American silver dollars. Look at the years."

My mouth dropped open. The dates ranged from 1890 to 1898. "Whoa," was all I could manage.

"They're for your collection," Mom said. "You can't spend them."

"No way! Thanks!"

"Thank Grandma," Mom said.

"I will!" I ran to my room and tucked the coins into the small chest where I kept my collection. Suddenly I didn't have the energy to leave my room. I lay down, exhausted, and slept the sleep of the righteous hard worker.

Seán Dwyer has published several short stories in a variety of journals. He is preparing to publish a memoir, A Quest for Tears, and will soon publish his first novel, which won a Chanticleer Somerset Award for best novel. In his spare time, he teaches Spanish.

Left on the Shore

Marian Exall

Charles Adams ran away to sea at fifteen from the smallholding a few miles outside Waterford on which he and his six siblings were born and raised. He left a note in his mother's missal promising to send her a silk shawl from the Orient, but he journeyed no further than Liverpool. The seasickness that racked his body a few miles out of Cork had not featured in his visions of the roving life.

"Yer no use to me in that condition," said the cargo ship's captain, anticipating the heavier swells of the Bay of Biscay. He dismissed the lad with directions to a Merseyside pub frequented by expatriot Irish looking for work. Years of helping his da patch up horse tack and farm equipment led to a job with a firm of carriage makers. Charles later boasted that he built a ceremonial coach for the Lord Mayor of Liverpool, but already in the early years of the twentieth century, gilded carriages pulled by white horses were the stuff of fairy tales. By that time, Charles was blessed with a wife, Eva, a local girl with middle-class aspirations. At eighteen-month intervals, three more blessings arrived.

Charles continued to dream of a new life in a foreign land. He seized upon the idea of emigration to Canada, and he would not let it go. Eva resisted. While she recognized that life in Liverpool did not offer all she could have hoped, she remained cautious. At least here she knew the rules, knew her place and the place of everyone else, what was possible and what was not.

Charles worked on her constantly, using all his Gaelic charm.

"Evie, me darlin', just think of the opportunities for the children: a new world. No steppin' aside when the gentry pass. *We'd* be the gentry."

Eva was unimpressed by his hyperbole. "Stepping aside" was not the problem—money was. Money translated into status. Status meant moving up, looking down, and having someone to look down on. In Liverpool, she had people to look down on. Not a huge population, it was true, but in Canada, who knew where the social lines were drawn?

She protested that her widowed mother could not spare her. When Charles insisted her mother could come too, knowing the old lady would fly to the moon before she would leave Merseyside, Eva came up with another excuse: she was with child again, their fourth. But Charles was on a mission. He laid siege with a determination he rarely sustained in other endeavors.

The Liverpool press covered the fitting out of the *Titanic*, the new star of the White Star Line. Her maiden voyage to New York was scheduled for April 1912. Charles brought home a brochure describing the Grand Staircase, the Turkish bath, the saltwater swimming pool, and the Promenade Deck at the bow, glassed-in to protect passengers from the spray.

Eva sniffed, "Hmm. I don't expect the steerage passengers have such luxury. They're probably stacked on top of each other; no chance to see the sky or breathe fresh air for the whole voyage."

Charles countered her argument, drawing attention to the pictures of the third-class promenade decks, fore and aft. "See! She's first class from top to bottom!"

Eva pointed out that the *Titanic* was to set sail from Southampton, not Liverpool, bound for New York, not Canada. Charles perceived a weak spot in her position. "Ah, well, if that's all ye're worried about! Won't it be worth a little train ride at either end to enjoy the maiden voyage of the *Titanic!*"

"What about your seasickness, Charles?" A low blow: Charles's brief career as a sailor was famous. Although happy to tell the tale against himself at family gatherings, he balked at having it brought up now.

"Evie, this ship is so advanced in design that you won't even know ye're at sea. Ye'll be as comfortable as if in yer own parlor."

"I wasn't thinking of *my* comfort," she responded dryly.

Charles did not give up. He dropped nuggets of information about the *Titanic* or Canada into conversation, no matter the topic. Eva would sigh, but not respond.

Charles earned enough to cover the essentials: rent, food, clothes, and the occasional treat like a day out to the seaside. But they had little left over. Eva, a careful housekeeper, took possession of his Friday wages, handing him back five shillings to do with as he pleased. She deposited anything she could save into a Post Office Savings Account, each payment and the slowly increasing balance dutifully recorded in the

Book, which she then hid away in the kitchen table drawer. These savings were for a rainy day, the disaster Eva expected from one moment to the next.

One evening in March, Eva proudly showed Charles the new balance: thirty-three pounds! He was impressed.

"How do you do it? Ye're a marvel! Just think what we can do with that much money!"

"It's not for spending!" Eva sternly replied, and tucked the Book out of sight before Charles could come up with ideas on how her hard-won safety net could be frittered away.

Charles already knew what to do with the money. Tickets for two adults and three young children in third class on the *Titanic* cost eighteen pounds, leaving more than enough for the train fares at either end and to see them set up in Toronto. Or, if they sold their furniture, and anything else they couldn't take with them, he could spring for second-class tickets at twenty-seven pounds. Yes, that would be best! Eva would never go for the segregated sleeping quarters in steerage, women and children separate from the men. And going second class would be a symbol of their new beginning: moving up in the world!

He made his plan. He'd withdraw the money from the Post Office and purchase the tickets on Monday, sorting out the rest of the details—the train to Southampton, a place to stay there before boarding the ship—as soon as he could. He'd announce the voyage as a *fait accompli* the following Friday, leaving more than a week to work out his notice—he was confident the chaps at work would organize a whip-round for him. Then they'd sell off their furniture, and say good-bye to friends and family before boarding the train for Southampton on April ninth.

The clerk at the White Star ticket office was helpful. He provided Charles with a copy of the railway timetable so that he could work out the times of the trains to Southampton. He even gave him the name and address of a respectable boarding house near the docks where they could spend their last night on English soil. Charles wrote to reserve a room immediately.

Things might have gone differently if Eva had not decided to make a deposit into the savings account on Friday, instead of Saturday morning when she customarily made the trip to the Post Office. Or if Charles had not stopped off at the pub for some Dutch courage before coming home, knowing he had an uphill job ahead of him. He was unprepared for the storm of shrill invective that greeted him at the front door. Eva didn't care for once what the neighbors might think.

"You stupid, lying, drunken piece of shite! You've pissed away your children's future. Everything I've slaved for!" She waved the Book in his face, then beat him around the head with it.

It took Charles several seconds to regroup. He had never heard such language from his wife, and the buffeting prevented him from responding. Eventually, he secured her wrists and brought her face to face with him.

"No, I've *saved* the children's future! I've bought us a passage to America on the *Titanic*!" If he thought this would calm the storm, he was, as in virtually everything, mistaken.

"I know what you did!" she snarled, and, freeing a hand, pointed at a letter lying on the hall table. The boarding house in Southampton had responded promptly, confirming a reservation for one night. "We are *not* going!"

To the neighbors' satisfaction, the row continued into the night, but the winner was a foregone conclusion. Before she would let him into the bedroom, Eva extracted a promise from Charles that he would obtain a refund for the tickets. They fell asleep exhausted, back to back, clutching the outer edges of the mattress in an effort not to accidentally touch each other in the night.

When Charles re-entered the White Star office, the clerk, so helpful before, adopted a superior air. "You've left it too late for a full refund. I can only give you ten percent back." He softened a little when he saw Charles's despair. "Look, why don't you hold on to the tickets? There are boats leaving for America all the time, and from Liverpool too. I can work out some kind of exchange, a passage on the *Adriatic*, the *Teutonic*, even on the *Titanic* herself, later in the year when the weather's better, and you've had a chance to settle things with your wife."

Thus, Charles secured a shred of hope, a dream of restored pride: he would gradually reintroduce the idea of emigration, and perhaps, when the baby was born, he could persuade her.

As he put up his tools at the end of the week, he thought of how he had imagined his co-workers slapping his back, wishing him luck, and envying him as he left the carriage works for the final time. It was hardly surprising that instead of returning to the house where all that awaited him was a scowl and a sharp inquiry about the ticket refund, he stopped at the pub instead.

Charles purchased his Guinness and looked around the room. He hailed the men he knew, and they hailed him. He was glad that, uncharacteristically, he had not boasted about his plans to sail to America on the *Titanic*. He pulled out the ticketing receipt and read it through again, before refolding it with a sigh and replacing it in an inside pocket. Staring into the dregs of his second pint, reality set in. Evie would never agree to emigrate. He could continue to dream, but could no longer delude himself that dreams came true.

Eva experienced her own epiphany while waiting for Charles to come home. She continued to nurse her week-long resentment as she readied the children for bed, but once she had them settled and sat down in the kitchen, she suddenly felt afraid. What if he went to Canada on his own? What if she had driven him away with her penny-pinching, her bourgeois pretensions, her fear of what others thought? His adoration of her, his amazement at her mundane accomplishments, elevated her from ordinary to exceptional. She could not do without him.

When Charles arrived home, she met him inside the front door, proffering her cheek for a kiss. Charles beamed and started to speak but Eva talked over him.

"Come and get your tea. I've been keeping it warm for you."

* * *

Eva heard about the *Titanic* first. On Tuesday, April sixteenth, she left the children with her mother for the afternoon while she went shopping. A newspaper placard shouted "*Titanic sinks! Thousands drown!*" She bought a paper, and hurried to the carriage works, where she waited outside the gate until Charles emerged at half past five to see her tear-stained face. He took the paper from her wordlessly and read it as they walked home together.

Marian Exall, Charles Adams' granddaughter, is his only descendant to fulfill the dream of emigration. Born and raised in England, Exall lived in France and Belgium before coming to the United States. She moved to Bellingham after a career as an employment lawyer in Atlanta, Georgia. She has published three mystery novels.

Soaring

Connie Feutz

In May 1948, a slender, petite brunette stood outside Room 500 of the Daniel Boone Hotel in Columbia, Missouri, nervously smoothing her skirt. Gathering her courage, she knocked on the door. "Hello. I'm Dorothy Jean Estep from the *Columbia Daily Tribune*. I'm here to interview Mr. Errol Flynn. May I please come in?"

Dorothy dreamt of one day writing for a major daily newspaper. Since high school she had worked for the *Columbia Daily Tribune*. Now in her third year at the University of Missouri in Columbia—one of the top journalism schools in the country—her editor, that morning, had given her a plum assignment, the scoop of her young life. Errol Flynn, the Hollywood Golden Age Screen Idol, Robin Hood himself, had surreptitiously swooped into her small college town atop forested hills and rolling prairies. Dorothy had rushed to the hotel.

As she was ushered into the room by Peter Stackpole, staff photographer for *Life* magazine, she saw Mr. Flynn—his lanky frame and burnished hair—hunched over a sink in the corner, shaving brush in one hand, razor in the other. He turned his handsome, lathered face toward her, gave her a grin, and kept shaving.

Flynn's charm and affability were legendary, as was his love of drink, cocaine, and underage women.

Dorothy pulled out her pad and pencil. Her story about the "filmland idol [who] had come to roost at the Daniel Boone Hotel," appeared the next day—front page news in the *Columbia Tribune*.

The debonair actor would slip out of Columbia early the next morning, and his life would continue along its well-established trajectory: more movies, more scandals, a third marriage. But for this young, ambitious reporter, his impulsive appearance in Columbia, Missouri, altered the course of her life.

A week after her piece about Errol Flynn ran in the *Columbia Tribune*, Dorothy received a telegram from *Life* magazine in New York City, inviting her to work for them for the summer. Ecstatic, Dorothy rushed to show her editor and mentor, Mr. Hamel.

A slight, bespectacled man, Jack Hamel read the telegram and handed it back to her. "Dorothy Jean," he said, "there is no reason for you to go to New York. You have a good job right here until you get married. You're meant to be someone's wife. Not a career woman."

Within a matter of moments, those few words—spoken so calmly, so dispassionately—had swept her delirious joy to the wayside. She stood stunned, filled with doubts. Dorothy turned and left the newsroom. Outside, beneath a brilliant and sanguine sky, she strode toward a wooded area where as an adolescent she had sought solace when her parents were arguing about her father's affair, a struggle that ultimately ended in their divorce. The father—who had called her his bluebird, who had taught her how to play bridge and tennis, whose eyes shone whenever he saw her—suddenly vanished, moving to a different state to marry this other woman. As she walked, Dorothy took no notice of the crimson redbuds, of the wild plums cloaked in white blossoms or of the melodic chatter of nearby songbirds. Still grasping the telegram, she felt torn—torn between loyalty and security on the one hand, adventure and possibility on the other. Mr. Hamel's opinion meant so much to her. Should she stay and remain working for the *Tribune*? Maybe she really wasn't good enough for *Life*. Or should she risk offending her editor and instead nurture this fragile ember of a dream of hers?

Thick, dark clouds had gathered. Heavy pellets of rain fell. Exhausted and confused, still with no real answers, she rushed to the small student boarding house where she rented a room, just as it began to downpour. On the front porch she ran into another student resident, Fritz Feutz.

"Quite the toad-strangler of a rain, wouldn't you say?"

Dorothy didn't know Fritz well; she'd hardly spoken to him. She turned her head so he wouldn't see she had been crying.

"Great job scoring the Flynn story, Dorothy!" Fritz knew Dorothy was the *Tribune* reporter who scored the first interview with Errol Flynn. Everyone in town knew that. When she didn't respond, her back still to him, he said, "Hey, is everything okay?"

Biting her lip, Dorothy handed Fritz the telegram.

His eyes grew large. "Whoa! *Life* magazine! No kidding! Congratulations!"

Dorothy avoided his gaze. "My editor told me I shouldn't take the job. He wants me to stay in Columbia. To stay at the *Tribune*." Dorothy paused, her voice softer. "Maybe it's just his way of telling me he doesn't think I'm up to it."

"Well now, I don't know your editor and I don't mean him any disrespect. But . . . I think he's just plain wrong. *Life* magazine! In New York City. Are you kidding me? What an opportunity. How could you say no to something like that? Who knows when it will ever come your way again."

"I don't know . . . *Life* magazine? Wanting *me*?!"

Fritz waved the Western Union telegram still in his hand. "Yes, you. *Life* magazine knows what they're doing, Dorothy."

He stared at her with an expression both defiant and tender. The dark-eyed girl tilted her head and looked up at the tall, lean man in front of her, his sable hair cut short. His enthusiasm washed over her, giving her unexpected comfort. He believed in her. Here was someone who actually encouraged her dreams. With a deep breath and a broad smile, she said, "You're right. They do know what they're doing. By God, I am going to take this job. I'm going to New York City; I'm going to work for *Life*!"

Fritz grinned. "Now, that's the spirit! You should be celebrating. C'mon, I'll take you out to dinner. Heck, I'll even fly you to St. Louis to catch your flight to New York."

Emil Feutz, aka Fritz, an aeronautical engineering student, also worked as a flight instructor and crop duster, and though Dorothy could not have known this, he welcomed any reason to pilot an airplane into the skies.

Early one morning a few days later, they drove to the local regional airstrip where Fritz, wearing dark aviator glasses, pointed out their airplane, a single-engine Stinson Gullwing, pale yellow with gray trim. He tossed her suitcase into the back and helped her on board. Once both were strapped in, Fritz cried out to the ground crew, "Clear prop!" and started the engine.

Her first time ever in an airplane, Dorothy was not prepared for the sudden clamor and shuddering as the propeller ramped up and they taxied down the grass runway. At takeoff, she sat bolt upright, gripping her seat. Fritz circled over Columbia, pointing out their boarding house, the *Tribune* building, the Daniel Boone Hotel. Her entire world was suddenly miniature, diminished, the streets a perfect grid, the cars so very tiny, people moseying along through their little lives while she gazed down from the gracefully banking airplane. She felt a tug, a recognition, that she was now leaving that world behind, for places unknown.

Beyond Columbia, the Stinson Gullwing soared over the colorful, quilted landscape of forest, fields, farms, and broad rivers. Dorothy felt the flush of excitement, of entering an entirely new world. By the time they touched down at the St. Louis Lambert airfield, she was smitten with this intelligent and spirited pilot.

* * *

In the fall of 1948, Dorothy returned to Columbia, to her last year at the university, to her job at the *Tribune*, to the same boarding house, eager to see Fritz again. To her disappointment, Fritz was friendly, though not interested in dating, not her nor seemingly anyone else. At the end of the school year, Fritz left Columbia for a summer job crop dusting.

Dorothy graduated in June 1949 with two declined marriage proposals and numerous job offers—including one from *Life* magazine. Though the pace and intensity of New York City had not suited her, she had enjoyed Philadelphia. So when *The Philadelphia Inquirer* offered her a job, she said yes. She was waiting until after her best friend's wedding in August, where she was the maid of honor, before leaving for Philadelphia.

In the receiving line at the wedding, wearing an orchid-pink strapless dress, Dorothy turned, surprised to see the next person in line was Fritz. Unbeknownst to her, the groom—who lived in their same boarding house—had invited him. But she was even more astounded when Fritz put his hands on her shoulders and warmly kissed her. It wasn't unwelcome; it was just so uncharacteristic of him, this public demonstration of affection.

In the days that followed, Fritz actively pursued her. They played tennis; they picnicked; they danced to "Night and Day by Bing Crosby. Fritz was warm and affectionate, yet mysteriously vague about visiting Dorothy in Pennsylvania. At the end of the week, he left for Illinois to return to crop dusting. Dorothy's suitcase was packed and ready for her move to Philadelphia.

On her second-to-last night in the *Columbia Tribune* newsroom, Dorothy saw an Associated Press wire with news that a plane had gone down near LaSalle, Illinois. A crop duster named Emil Feutz had been pulled out from the wreckage with serious burns. Dorothy immediately called the *La Salle News Tribune* and learned that Fritz had been taken to a nearby hospital in Peru, Illinois.

Dorothy Jean Estep didn't own a car nor had she ever driven out of Boone County. But by dawn the next day, Dorothy was on the road in a borrowed car determined to see Fritz. The three-hundred-mile journey took her seven hours.

Arriving at the hospital, she blithely told the staff she was his sister. They told her he had not broken any bones, although he had suffered severe burns on his arms and legs. A nurse led her to a room where she found Fritz swathed in bandages.

He managed a weak smile when he saw her. "So, Miss Dorothy Jean Estep. Just what brings you to this neck of the woods? Is Errol Flynn in the next room?"

Dorothy cracked a smile. "Oh dear God, Fritz. What happened?"

He described how he had been spraying corn borers when he became distracted trying to not dust the farmers in the nearby fields. The tip of a wing had caught a telephone cable.

They talked of this and that, when Fritz—who, as a WWII veteran, had one more year of college—blurted, "Well, Dorothy Jean. Would you like to get married before school starts in a couple of weeks? Or wait until Thanksgiving?"

She stared at the man before her, still good-looking even in the ragged state he was in. Perhaps even more so. Her heart pulsed in her throat. "Are you serious?"

He smiled, squeezed her hand, and nodded. "I know being a pilot's wife isn't the most glamorous prospect you've ever been offered. But it sure would make this ol' Mizzoura boy mighty happy to have you at his side."

"My, my, my." She struggled to catch her breath. She knew she yearned to be with this enigmatic man. In her brief twenty-three years, Dorothy had lived through the Great Depression, a World War, and having her father walk out on her family. Errol Flynn inexplicably "had come to roost" in her local town, followed by the opportunity to work in New York City and now this terrifying accident. Dorothy was acutely aware of how the unexpected, how happenstance, can dramatically alter the course of one's life. If they waited three long months, why anything could happen. Anything. Why, Fritz could even change his mind. "Well, Mr. Emil Feutz, I think I might like that idea . . . Why yes, let's do it. Before school starts."

* * *

Dorothy and Fritz wed on September 18, 1949, and were married for sixty-six years, until Fritz died at the age of ninety.

Connie Feutz was named after an airplane—the Lockheed Constellation, or the "Connie." Fritz attained his dream and was hired as a test pilot for Cessna in 1950. Dorothy continued working as a journalist until she became pregnant with their second child. Connie lives and writes in Bellingham, Washington.

A Sailboat Named Desire

Lula Flann

I'd cruised before, scores of times, in these very seas. The wide Sargasso, to be specific. That March, the watery plains were scarcely riffled. Cerulean skies floated above, untroubled by anything more ominous than cloud frills and contrails. Ill winds might blow, say, a marriage to the shoals. Our ship glided away from dock, bands played, confetti flew, and boo- ties shook. It didn't seem like the kind of day when worlds get rocked. But if all it takes is a stiff wind, or a stiff drink, or a stiffie of any sort — isn't a marriage bound to go down sooner or later?

I noticed the blonde as she stepped aboard. Not that there was any reason to. She walked conventionally pretty in a sea of extraordinary. She stood silent while the Amazonian, the petite, the gorgeous, the outrageous and the proudly unadorned swirled around her, women cascading into their different pools of energy. From a distance, she was ordinary and alone, outstanding only for the taut jaw signaling terror, the high, tight shoul- ders, sensitive to a sign — any sign, that would spur her to spring off the gangway. As it was, she blindsided me, taking a hasty left up the center stairwell.

"Forgive me!" I swayed, and tried to read the name tag of the handsome woman I'd just clipped.

"I always say, act first, ask forgiveness later." She fluttered her own name tag at me. "Looks like we're both on board as staff. I'm Elle."

"I'm Em." This was the moment to walk it all back, but. But the moment I stepped on deck, a phantasm of pheromones waved to life, right there, *underneath my clavicle. I waved off the first lesbian I'd ever officially met, and fled toward my cabin. My inner compass, something I'd not suspected possessing, swiveled due North. My panties were swamped by a swell. I was the lone het girl on an all-Sapphic ship. The soft shoulders I bumped as I shifted directions and winnowed my way below decks were heretofore only the stuff of dreams and well-fingered erotica.*

I set sail aboard this ship a married woman and mother of many. My spouse had kissed me good-bye and encouraged me to eat pussy on his behalf while I was on this business trip. For a guy who went to church three times a week, he had a significant relationship with Hustler *and glossy girl-on-girl tropes. He and I had laughed as he drove me to the airport. I'd like to say he had no one to blame but himself. His sentiment of spousal generosity proved prescient when I returned ashore two weeks after crossing the Rubicon, ready for my walking papers. I'd like to say he knew what I knew pretty much as soon as I knew it. Immediacy of revelation did not count for as much as I thought it should.*

A stiff estrogen breeze blew through the corridors, sex sounded from behind closed doors, prow to bow to

mizzen and back again. The ship sailed full of folk singers and funky beats, hellions, hale from the twenty-
years' post-Stonewall wars and fresh young femmes
taking their first dance steps with a beloved high on the
aft deck. Women sniffed their fingers and smiled. These
were my mates. I watched her spy on them from the end
of a bar. She was trying to secret her five-foot-eight
frame behind a paperback and the first of several tall gin
and tonics. She scrutinized her fellow voyagers from the
front row of line dance classes. I led them all to shouts
of, "Bend down, turn around and do-si-do." I worked
the cruise, too, as a dance instructor this time around.

Later in the trip, she, this long, lean, odd woman out,
would side-eye those same lesbians from the guide seat
of a shore excursion bus. There, she traded aloofness for
tour leader efficiency. She was largely forgettable, that
average blonde, except for the fear I smelled on her.
That was the beginning of the week. The musky schvitz
was memorable.

By the middle of the week, I could only smell her fear
during the slow dances. During the nightclub two-step,
I ruminated about the fact that we are an altruistic lot.
The woman and her unusual status were curiosities.
There were couples aboard, and there were women
aboard without partners, but this particular woman—
this straight woman, was at that tipping point most of
us had either been in or helped folks out of.

As the week progressed, I realized she had a nice
smile. A genuine smile. A warm smile. I wondered what
books she was reading as she drank her G&Ts. I started
to think: she's going to make it with someone. You want
to make sure that the first experience is the right experience. I'm sorry to say that kind of thing can't be

entrusted to just anyone. Who better than someone she doesn't know? And she doesn't know Jill-of-all-trades, good-with-her-hands, always-ready-to-step-away, me.

I embarked as one person and got off as another. I boarded the ship loving women in the abstract. I stepped foot onboard knowing there were women in the world who wielded power-ful pens, forged trails in their chosen fields, women who stepped into lives apart from the lives spent in luncheons and parent-teacher meetings. I was at sea among a boatload of women brave enough to inhabit their day to day in the com-pany of someone other than the Man. That's the way I summarized and simplified the world's hierarchies then. It was all so very straightforward. I truly did believe.

I'd been winning for an hour. That hour had followed the hour it took for the ship to cross into international waters. The gamine croupiers unlocked the casino doors to a line of blackjack-playing babes. The lamb eventually appeared at my elbow. I gave her the time of day.

"You play?"

"No—I just want to watch."

I'm sure she did. Just want to watch. Easier to be a by-stander than a player.

"First time?" Like I hadn't heard word around the deck. Like I hadn't put down money with some of the others that wouldn't be the case for long. She smelled good, and I liked that she had William Carlos Williams tucked under her arm. I used to have a girlfriend who asked me to read that to her while she set up camp for us. Now that she was closer, I saw something about her that I'd sensed but not seen from across the dance floor, across the pool deck. She was in her head. We could change that. No skin off my nose.

"Original thinkers." I mouthed the words as I stepped back from the roulette table to the empty backgammon tray behind me. I fingered the quartz rounds. My nipples were just that hard. I drank up the ease, the confidence, the swagger of the gamblers around me. I could draft behind them. The ubiquitous Them. The ones who came before. That's only fair . . . there are plenty who had already tried their luck at drafting me into their ranks. "Come on over to this side," the sirens sang. "Lash yourself to the mast if you like. You get to say what you want, do what you want, be with whom you want." Wildly simplistic, those sirens. No doubt what Odysseus thought, too. What's in a name? I listened to the clatter of the ball on the spinning roulette wheel, recited their names to its clickatat: Pisinoe *translates as* "Persuasive Mind," Thelxiepeia—*if I could just say it—heralds* "Soothing Words," Aglaophonos *means "Beautiful Voice,"* Thelxiope *signifies "Persuasive Face."* Teles *is code for "Perfect." She'd said her name was Elle, but it seemed more likely she was one of those named by Homer. This one in front of me could be any of those. Still, what did I care what name she went by? I carefully replaced the rounds on the backgammon board and drifted toward the woman at the roulette wheel.*

"Anyone waiting for you at home?" No point beating around the bush. Rumor was mixed on this point, and knowing the answer would decide if I put the next move on even, odd, or let it ride. She didn't wear the Mardi Gras beads indicating she sailed as a single. She didn't read as eager. Maybe I'd heard wrong. In that moment, she most reminded me of the sheep I'd lassoed during a demonstration shearing. Subdued. Estranged from herself.

"I have a family at home."

I raised my eyebrows.
"Who's in your family?"

"The usual. Husband. Kids."

Yes. Like that sheared sheep, she was curiously calm in the face of the shit storm that awaited. Maybe she thought the dude she was married to would be delighted to hear about her fabulously gay epiphany. You can sail the seven seas, but human nature will out. If this guy took the news different from all the others, he'd be one in a bazillion. Most men can't fathom that having a penis just means dick. Coming out as a lesbian wasn't as easy as falling off the top deck, even if this was the nineties.

(There once was a girl from the Midwest
Who didn't care what sort of Tempest
Her ideas ever wrought
Or her actions then brought
To the fine tribe of womyn most Queerest)

Her shadowed eyes checked the red ball as it riveted around the wheel. There's no safe harbor, and so much depends upon the kindness of a perfect stranger. I was the perfect stranger, and she was determined to roll the dice. If you're over thirty and you try your luck with the ladies, there's no going back.

I only knew her that once, but I'm pretty sure she never did. Go back.

Lula Flann, a devotee of head-turning ensembles and brilliant broads, writes Cozy-Noir from her Cascadian bungalow on the bay. Author of the Mata Morrow Mysteries, Lula is currently working on Carlotte's Compostela, *a re-telling of feminist fables rooted in the pre-history of the Camino Francés.*

Raised with Bush Devils

Shannon Hager

So much depends upon life's experiences to form and mold our outlook of the world. My name is Ayman and I am a teenage kid living in the West African bush country with my father. I want to tell you the story of how I came to believe in the unfathomable.

My Palestinian mother married my Lebanese father and they lived on her family's farm in Palestine. They had four children—my three sisters and me. In the late 1950s, the family's farm was taken for settlements by the young state of Israel. My mother, my sisters and I moved to a refugee camp in Lebanon, and my father emigrated to a small village deep in the bush country of West Africa. With the help of a cousin who had a business there, my father set up a shop and sold merchandise like kerosene, cigarettes, beer, cloth, toilet paper, batteries, and housewares to the people of the Bustup tribe. Every few years he returned to visit us for several months.

During my father's trip home in 1971, he said, "Son, it's time for you to learn about work and running the business." So, when he returned to West Africa, I went with him, full of curiosity about this place my father always called the "white man's grave."

My father and I lived fifty miles from the nearest other white person, in a stick-and-mud building much like our neighbors, but we had a zinc roof, whereas our neighbors' roofs were thatch. We slept and ate in a couple of rooms at the rear of the shop, and an old African man cooked for us in an outdoor kitchen behind our living quarters. We had no benefits of a civilized life like electricity, running water, or an indoor toilet. I stayed busy stocking the shelves and sweeping out the shop each morning before we opened.

I soon realized the dense jungle and steamy tropical environment concealed mystery and secrets. When I first learned about the Greta secret society for women, I laughed and thought they were witches. One day I saw a group of adolescent girls with their naked torsos covered in white paint with geometric designs. My father told me they were initiates into this women's secret society and lived in the forest where they were taught tribal secrets. I stared at them because they seemed so ridiculous in their grass skirts that shook like ballerina tutus when they strolled past the shop. I shouted "little witches" in Arabic at them.

My father smacked me hard on my head, almost knocking me to the floor. "You need to be more respectful of the traditional culture," he hissed.

I learned that at some point during their three or four years in this strange bush school, the girls were circumcised. Their clitorises were removed. At the time I didn't know what that meant. Nor did I know what else might have been done to them during this procedure. My father told me the girls were cut to keep them from getting pleasure out of sex and becoming too "frisky" or promiscuous. That seemed pretty severe to me. Later I discovered this practice happens in many African cultures and causes numerous problems with infections and childbirth, but as a teenage boy, this mutilation of young females was not my concern.

One evening as darkness descended with the sunset, I left the shop to light the kerosene lamp in our living quarters. It was one of those adjustments to living without electricity that I did as a matter of routine, almost without thought. However, this evening when the lamp threw up its light, bats began flying in the unscreened windows, diving at me and making meowing sounds like kittens. For some reason I was sure they were sent by the Greta bush society women in retaliation for all the teasing and mean things I had said about the girls. I had laughed at stories about the women's ability to control nature and the magic acts they performed, but I was not laughing now. I was frightened beyond reason and was quickly developing a new respect for the African supernatural. I blew out the lamp and dove under the table to get away from the bats swooping around my head.

Fearfully, I waited in the darkness, listening to endless insect noises of the living African night and watching bats zoom across the room in the iridescent glow of the moonlight. I desperately wanted those bats to go away, yet I was fascinated.

When the last of the bats flew out the window into the claustrophobic forest, I was about to pee in my pants from fear.

I was too ashamed to talk to my father about what happened. I told myself I imagined it all, that I had had one too many sips of that bush-made sugarcane juice smelling like turpentine that my father sold from a large bottle sitting on the counter by the cash register.

Several days later a small boy told me the bush girls wanted to "catch me." I asked what the hell that meant. He said they wanted to take me to the bush, then shrugged his shoulders when I asked what they would do with me. I was fearful of something I could not even imagine.

Sometimes the girls hung out in front of the store, looking at me and speaking Bustup together. They threw finger signs at each other and at me and then they would all burst out laughing. My anxiety level rose, and although I made no more jokes about the bush society girls, I was afraid to be alone in case they came for me. I was finally forced to talk about it with my father when I could no longer evade his questions concerning my anxious behavior.

My father told me that someone who was disrespectful towards these African beliefs in the supernatural could be "caught" and taken to the bush, never to be seen or heard from again. "Don't expect the government to intervene to get you back if you get 'caught,' " my father warned me. "Get used to African bush society business," he said. "You're going to have more experiences with that stuff if you continue to live in Africa. Just quit making fun of them."

What worried me was that people who were not a part of the female bush society, or the male version, appeared very afraid of these groups. Sometimes at night I could hear a flute playing, winding through the trees, first here, then there. The people told me this was the devil of the Kelt men's society playing enchanting music and looking for converts to take into the world of spirits.

The first time I heard this sound, the old cook warned me, "Go in the house, shut the windows and lock the door. Don't come out-o. And don't you be peeking!"

My father always closed the store when the devil moved about through the forest, but he left the back door to the yard open while the old cook made us dinner. When the old man finished cooking and placed the dishes on the table in the house, he closed the back door and left. The door was not opened again until the next morning when the cook returned.

In the months that followed, I saw great dancing devils of the Valé tribe, stomping and dancing and shaking rattles of beads and shells, looking as big and grassy as a Nebraska haystack I had seen in an old magazine from America. Painted men with leaves in their hair beat hollowed-out logs in hypnotizing rhythms and dust billowed up from the feet of the fierce dancing devils. Frightened people around me wanted the devils to go away and not take their children. I didn't want them to take me.

I never, ever entertained the idea of going swimming, even on the hottest days. Niege water spirits were said to live in underwater caves, and people disappeared when they got too close to these caves called "feeding grounds." Children were severely beaten if they didn't listen to their parents' warning about not swimming in the rivers.

Later, when my father and I had gone to the capital city for supplies, I saw seven men hung by the neck until dead for participating in ritualistic killings. This was during the time of the revolution when the government executed many people for coup plotting, including so-called witch doctors and bush devils charged with conspiracy to overthrow the government by making magic against its officials. During elections in peaceful times, "heart man murders" kept people inside at night. The belief was that when people disappeared, the devils cut their bodies up for parts to make strong "medicine." The heart was said to have special attributes for winning political positions. In some parts of Africa, people who practiced this were called "werewolves."

I found myself becoming more superstitious the longer I lived with the Africans. I came to believe in the power of supernatural acts to control nature. I believed the mind alters its thought process when caught up by bush magic. It is a reality that is as frightening as it is weird, but one that must be dealt with.

I adapted to all this supernatural mumbo-jumbo because I had no choice. I lived in the middle of it by not being curious about what was going on—it was not safe for me to know about such things. To keep my head on straight when bush magic started to mess with my mind, I got out the broom and swept the shop, or dusted and restocked the shelves. And I always, always, made sure to close the windows after dark.

Shannon Hager, author of the award-winning memoir Five Thousand Brothers-in-Law: Love in Angola Prison, *is finishing her second book,* Attitude Adjustments: The Struggle Continues, *the story of a clueless woman living through riots and revolution in a West African country.*

The Crown

Jolene Hanson

On a November morning in 1985, we piled our belongings onto sleds and dragged them through the snow to the family car, a Scout Traveler half-eaten by rust. Mom balanced a seven-month-old on her hip while Dad arranged large items like beds and chairs in the back of his pickup truck. Commands were barked, tears shed, and in the end—papers, old toys, and a few unwashed clothes lay scattered throughout rooms in the little yellow farmhouse, the detritus of five interrupted childhoods.

I did not understand the permanence of the word *foreclosure* when I was eight years old—that we could never come back and that our livestock, tractors, and even our beat-up swing set were gone forever. So, when we drove away that day, I didn't cry over the red barns or hollow corn silo, the farmhouse, or sleeping cornfields shrouded in white. I didn't cry over our two dogs running through belly-deep snow, howling after the Scout until the wind chased them back into a barn. I assumed we would return.

Mom and Dad fought headwinds and near white-out conditions all the way to Glenwood, a one-stoplight town in the middle of Minnesota where both sets of grandparents lived. Set in a valley, Glenwood hugged the shores of Lake Minnewaska, a summer tourist destination that was now frozen and dotted with fish houses. Only locals remained in town, huddled around café bars, sipping cups of hot coffee and chatting up other displaced farmers about the evils of Reaganomics.

Our new home, a partially finished A-frame, sat at the top of a hill and had a million-dollar view of Glenwood. It was a bankrupt construction project that no one wanted to invest in during those bleak economic years, but Dad somehow managed to buy it with the promise of sweat-equity. It was barely more than the bones of a house with dirt floors and exposed studs. Stairs led to a second story with plywood floors. Dad gave us each a carpet square to sit on that first week before he found a couch.

I have no doubt my dad suffered for losing the farm and uprooting his family, but it was Mom who suffered most visibly that winter. Dad left the house every morning to fix farm machinery, and Mom stayed home with the kids. Not long after the New Year, she lost interest in cleaning. Dishes piled up on the table and in the sink, and trash collected in corners. She began drifting around the house in a purple bathrobe, reading romance novels and endlessly twirling the same piece of hair. Sometimes she'd read the *Pope County Tribune* and tell us about so-and-so who'd lost their farm or who'd celebrated a fiftieth wedding anniversary or died the past week.

I feared that, in a way, we'd lost Mom in the foreclosure too. But then, one summer morning in 1986 the fog lifted. Some ray of sunlight pierced through that darkness, and Mom got dressed. She got in the Scout and drove away with such unprecedented excitement, we had to wonder if she'd ever come back. Five nose prints dirtied the glass waiting for her to return, and when she finally did a half hour later, she ran up the stairs with a copy of the newspaper in hand.

"Jolene!" she called, out of breath, face glowing and brown eyes alight. "I entered you in the Junior Waterama Queen pageant. There were only twelve spots, and you got in!" She pushed dishes aside and opened the paper across the kitchen table. There was my picture, along with eleven other candidates. We all crowded around, trying to get a good look.

Glenwood Waterama was an annual festival held the last weekend of July. It started on a Thursday, extending through the weekend with various activities that culminated with the crowning of a Junior Waterama Queen and Princess. The town's new royalty would represent Glenwood all over the state for an entire year, attending pageants and riding in parades on top of a nautical-themed float. Most little girls in Pope County dreamed of wearing the queen's velvet robe and coveted diamond tiara. Mom had never entered me before because we'd lived on the farm, and there had been work to do. But now . . .

I studied my photo and those of the other candidates. In my first moment of real insecurity, I noticed Kimberly Busch's perfect white smile and Hollie Johnsrud's delicate doll-like face.

"Mom, I'm the only one with freckles."

"That's good! You'll stand out."

"I have a butt chin." I pressed my thumb into the slight depression, surprised that I'd never noticed it before. My face now displayed next to eleven others, my imperfections seemed so glaring.

"It's a dimple, not a butt chin. Brigitte Bardot has a chin dimple."

That brought me no comfort.

Mom and I went shopping and found a pale pink dress at a secondhand shop for ten dollars. It had long sleeves and a square, white lace collar. Completing the outfit was a pair of jelly shoes in a matching shade of pink, purchased at the Corner Drugstore for one dollar. The night before the pageant, Mom sat on the bed next to me and wound strands of wet, strawberry blond hair into circles that she secured to my head with bobby pins. As she worked, she coached me on sitting up straight—good posture would score points with the judges—and saying please and thank you.

Mom removed the bobby pins in the morning, and my dry hair unwound into curls. She brushed them out and pinned back the sides. We didn't have a full-length mirror, so I ran outside to admire the completed ensemble and hairdo in the reflection of a window. I practiced waving to imaginary crowds like Princess Diana. I spun on the heels of my jelly shoes, digging holes in the dirt and watching my dress twirl. Mom must have shot a whole roll of film documenting my last morning as a commoner.

The judging would take place at the Minnewaska House, an upscale restaurant by the lake. Mom drove me there, providing last-minute coaching reminders. Assured of victory, I bounced out of the car and skipped to the door . . . and then stopped dead in my tracks. All the other girls sashayed into the banquet room wearing fine lace gowns with puffy sleeves and patent leather shoes. Bows and glittering barrettes adorned dramatic bouffants and cascading spiral curls. Suddenly, I felt like a dandelion in a bed of roses. Several girls stopped to stare at me, eyeing my jelly shoes and long-sleeved dress that could have easily belonged to one of their older sisters at one time. My cheeks flushed with embarrassment.

I tried approaching a couple of the girls I knew, but they closed their circle when I drew near, denying me entry. I was too shy to approach the ones I didn't know. So I turned to go back outside. Maybe Mom was still there? Even if not, I'd sit on the curb and wait for her to come back.

"What a beautiful dress," a woman said to me before I could escape. "Why don't you come sit over across from me at the table? Lunch is about to start."

I followed the woman back into the banquet room. She was one of three judges, and over lunch, they took turns asking us questions about ourselves like, do you have any pets? Or, how many brothers and sisters do you have? I remembered to say please and thank you, to put my napkin on my lap, and to keep my elbows off the table. I made eye contact and sat up straight. When I got up to leave later, I told them, "Nice to meet you." Just as Mom coached me.

Afterward, the queen candidates paired up and rode on the back of convertibles down Main Street, waving at throngs of people lined up along a parade route that ended at Glenwood's band shell. In front of the band shell were dozens of rows of benches, already filling with residents and summer visitors. Across the street by the lake were vendor booths with bags of cotton candy, games, and foot-long hotdogs.

The clouds began to gray, and the air thickened with heat and humidity. One by one, we were called onto the stage. My curls had all but straightened by the time I walked out to wave at the crowd. The long sleeves of my dress began to itch; the material didn't breathe, and I was sweating. After, I took a seat on stage next to the other candidates, fanned around the current Junior Queen and Princess.

Singers and dancers glided across the stage before the winners were announced. And there I was in the middle of lace and ruffles and patent leather shoes and hairspray, suddenly hoping I didn't win because I didn't want to draw any more attention to myself in my secondhand dress and droopy hair. Winning felt like something you could reach up and grab hold of . . . and just as easily release. What if I just let it go? But then I looked down at my mother, sitting in the front row, and her smile was so big, and dimples so deep. I knew she wanted it more than I did, and she wanted it so badly. That's not to say I didn't want to win. I liked the idea of winning. But I mostly just wanted to have a crown for the novelty of it and then maybe go home and read some books.

"Holly Beck!" The name of the Junior Princess had just been announced. The audience clapped and whistled as blonde-haired, blue-eyed Holly rose to wave at them. Mom's face fell. I knew what she was thinking — that only meant one more chance. However, I also knew that princess wouldn't have been good enough. She would complain all year about how I'd have been a better queen and how it's all rigged for the rich anyway. The only two options were to either lose entirely or win completely. But when I looked at her face, I knew I had to win. Losing would break something inside of her. In a world of constant babies and food stamps and a foreclosed farm home that she missed like crazy, she needed this moment more than I did. She needed something to look forward to. If I won, she'd get to curl my hair once or twice a week, and she could visit new places around the state and take pictures of me in parades and tell any one who would listen that *her* daughter was The Queen.

Jill Blair, the current Junior Waterama Queen, took to the podium wearing a blue velvet robe with a white feather collar. Her hair had been ratted and sprayed to eighties perfection, and a rhinestone crown sparkled above the sharp spikes of brown hair. She opened the envelope and pulled out a slip of paper.

Silence.

"Jolene Hanson!"

A thousand faces turned in my direction, but there was only one that mattered as I got up to take my place in Waterama history. Mom took copious pictures as I knelt by the podium, shaking with nervous excitement, and Jill Blair placed the velvet robe over my shoulders. Then, she lifted a brand-new tiara from a box. Rhinestones sparkled just like real diamonds across a silver headband. Placed upon my head, a warm current of pride transformed my rags into riches.

For over thirty years now, Mom has been the keeper of my crown and, more importantly, the memories of that summer. Those memories are self-made treasures without legal titles or deeds, the only things either of us could ever truly possess.

Jolene Hanson writes memoir and blogs about her frequent travels to Ireland. Her essays have appeared locally in Whatcom WRITES! *anthologies and in* Southside Living. *She also enjoys storytelling through pictures, and has a growing portfolio on JoleneHansonPhotography.com*

What Remains

Sky Hedman

My easygoing and likeable younger brother, John, was a collector. Or was he a hoarder?

The little boy who I remember in knee pants grew up and married his wife, Jeanne, when they were both teenagers. They began their life together in a clapboard country house in a rural area of New Jersey. As they filled up their house with three children, he also filled it up with found treasures: bicycles in need of repair, scraps of wood, red wagons, rusty snow shovels, and ATVs. Over the years, his collection also filled their garage, and then spilled into the side yard. When Jeanne put up a fuss, he built a wooden stockade fence around his stuff. Soon the tips of the objects peeked out over the top of the fence, and their acre took on the allure of a not so thinly veiled junkyard.

John's best find was a huge clown head on a twenty-foot pole, complete with red curly hair and a big red nose. The red hat was somewhat faded and his facial features were no longer vibrant, but still, he caught my eye and I wondered about his past life as he leaned his head against the garage in rain, sun, and snow.

To John and Jeanne, the neighborhood went down when the wooded acreage behind their house was sold and subdivided. Someone built a luxurious two-story home on the land that adjoined John's junkyard. The upstairs windows of the new home afforded his neighbors an excellent view down into his collection. The new owners complained. John responded by turning the clown around to face the neighbor's window, filling their view with the unrelenting stare of the clown's aging face.

We all had a good laugh, yet I was shocked at John's steadiness and lack of contrition about the effect of his junk on the new neighbor. I silently sympathized with the buyer, who had paid a high price to gain purchase in a quiet upscale subdivision. On every visit to John and Jeanne's, I delighted in riding bikes around the country lanes with them or rollerblading in the parking lot of a nearby church with the kids. I also noticed the creep of his growing collection. I imagined the stress of living near John or of being John's wife. Despite her efforts to contain his collecting, to mark off safe play spaces for their kids, to enhance the charm of their little house in the country, the collection that even John referred to as "John's junk" grew. As each of his secondhand cars or trucks reached the end of its functional life, it took up permanent residence in his back field.

"Just like Daddy," my siblings and I commented, lightheartedly referring to our father who had a similar propensity to stockpile things.

When I think of my generous and fun brother, a good father, a steady worker, I get it that he enjoyed the thrill of a good deal—picking objects up from trash or buying them cheap at an auction or yard sale. He didn't have equal energy for putting them to use or distinguishing the useless from the useful. He didn't have a plan for excess, such as a regular habit of going to a dump station or Goodwill. In fact, I would hesitate to suggest going to a garbage dump, since odds are he would come home with more than he brought.

Geographic miles separated me from my brother in our adult years. In that space, my objections to his collecting remained unspoken. My relationship with John coasted to a casual level, with our contact limited to occasional family reunions, usually celebrating another five years of our aging mother's life.

I was disappointed to learn that after thirty-three years of marriage, John and Jeanne's marriage had frayed beyond repair. The constant irritation of his collection was just one ingredient in their separation. John moved out to start a new life in rural West Virginia. His wife and much of his junk stayed behind. He intended to come back for his stuff. With John, there were a lot of intentions that didn't happen according to his predicted timeline.

I didn't want to label this accumulation of possessions as hoarding. When I finally did, I wrestled with the excuses and the contextual softening of the truth. I was aware that his collection took over the premises like well-nourished kudzu. I didn't yet recognize that his collecting was damaging to his human relationships. In retrospect, I must admit that his junk became overwhelming and paralyzing, creating a poisonous ecology for John, Jeanne, and their family, and for even the most generous souls of onlookers.

I wanted to be that most generous soul. I wanted to honor our shared human architecture. What sparked my heart? What motivated me? What brought me a spot of happiness?

I also felt the rush from finding something new to me, whether a good deal from my favorite thrift store or an overstocked chain store. I also carried around more stuff than was necessary, like the compost that my life partner, Lynne, and I moved from house to house when we were young adults or the extra Volkswagen engines that we held onto with the thought of future use.

John discouraged our extended family from visiting him in his new life in West Virginia. At the time, I didn't understand why he distanced himself from us, but I could guess that he wanted space from our potentially critical eyes. I spoke to him occasionally on the phone, and was happy to hear that he found a new partner, Sheila. I had a glimpse of the texture of their life when John told me that they had brought home a fawn that they found on the side of the road and, remarkably, were raising it in their house alongside their two rather frightening pit bulls. He sent pictures of the young deer eating out of its own dog food bowl in the kitchen, and sleeping on their bed. I was relieved when John said that it learned to use the dog door.

Sheila was a vintage antiques dealer, traveling the east coast living in a van, displaying her wares at various antique shows and flea markets. A match made in heaven, I thought, glad they had found each other.

John moved with Sheila to a small town in the mountains of Virginia, where they bought an old commercial building, which had at one time been River Street Hardware store. They set up shop to sell their wares on the first floor, making their new home upstairs in the apartment on the second floor. They shared a delight in found things. Eventually, Sheila and John filled up two more downtown commercial storefronts.

Over the shop's front door was a quirky and charming yellow sign that John made from his collection of *objets*. The sign slid in and out on a metal curtain rod with oak finials to display open in blue wooden letters. The wares were organized around a center aisle. Here were the cherry and oak trunks, wood side tables with inlay, tarnished brass lighting fixtures, Windsor chairs with broken spindles, fancy wrought iron hooks, and Hoosier kitchen cabinets. I was particularly delighted by the large pieces they snagged, which were displayed in a separate building. It had the allure of a museum with medieval suits of armor, the large armoire that needed a house with very high ceilings, the six-foot sparkly crystal chandelier perfect for a grand entry hall and the heavy banquet-sized dining room table that seated twenty, all of them remnants of a lavish architectural past.

On my first visit to the shop, I weaved and dodged to peruse the pieces on the periphery. I was stopped from browsing the adjoining storefront, the second half of the store, by signs marking keep out. This area of the store was closed off and served as a repository. These things weren't ready to be sold, were unsalable, were unsuitable, were set aside, a visual suggestion that John and Sheila were overwhelmed with the quantity of stuff they accumulated.

I understood "overwhelmed." I understood the result of being overwhelmed. Things dropped off my list when I got too busy. The things that dropped off John's list were cleanup, disposal, repair, reduction.

A year ago, John was diagnosed with pancreatic cancer and given twelve months to live. He was fifty-seven. His first thought was, "I still have so much to do." I thought then of their extensive collection and the unfinished remodeling of the old buildings and silently agreed. Lacking health insurance, his medical care took a rocky course, and was often delayed while his requests for Medicaid were tied up in the bureaucratic process. Alarmed at the rate that the cancer was spreading its ill effects, I offered to pay for his care when the process stalled, but he always refused. I heard one phrase repeatedly from my uncomplaining brother: "I'm okay."

I kept in touch with John over the phone, talking to him more frequently than I ever had. Even if he didn't answer right away, I loved hearing his gentle and good-natured voicemail greeting, cheerfully telling me to leave a message. I made three trips to Virginia, willing to accept whatever I found, traveling from Washington State to spend some time with him and to get to know Sheila. His diagnosis had re-opened the doors for communication with his children and grandchildren, who now were making an effort to come visit him. For all of us, we never knew which visit would be the last.

Even as the symptoms of his cancer robbed his vitality, John insisted on driving us around to show off picturesque mountainous overlooks. He took us out to breakfast when he no longer had an appetite. He rarely complained; instead, I had to quiz him about his symptoms, only finding out the details of the pain that he was masking by careful questioning. I ached because I wanted to, but could not, rescue him from this situation.

I encouraged him to move to my sister's small, clean one-story house in the same town for his final months, picturing peace and calm being away from his clutter and unfinished projects. I was frustrated but not surprised when he pushed back strongly, clearly stating that he wanted to stay the course, staying in the space that he and Sheila had created, amidst his own stuff, his stereo, his couch, his clocks, his treasures, in the high-ceilinged apartment fronting River Street.

John died last month. I ache for this loss, of his kind good nature, his generosity and his compassion for animals. Gone from this earth are his creativity and artistic sense. Gone is his amiable greeting, the brother who was always easy to talk to. He leaves behind children and grandchildren who will miss his simple delights.

John died as he had lived, upstairs over the antique store, with his partner, his two pit bulls and the cat at his side. Two of his grown children were with him, as well as our youngest sister. The broad staircase up to the second floor was decorated with eighteenth-century oil portraits in gilt frames that he had hung artfully on the tall walls. Each of the twenty-one steps had at least one treasure on it: a large piece of quartz, a pink granite rock, an iron tool, or a statue that he liked.

The hospital bed placed in the middle of the living room is gone, replaced by an urn and photos of John. My memories of this fun, easygoing, artistic, and independent brother fill my heart. I witnessed the beginning, middle, and end of his precious life. The clown face that stared down his neighbors still smiles in my memory. Collector or hoarder, my love for my brother remains.

Sky Hedman loves to write and tell stories, some of which can be found on her blog: SkyandLynne.blogspot.com. After several careers, including radio, engineering, and teaching, she is grateful to be mostly retired in Bellingham with her wife, Lynne. She works just enough for the Alaska Ferry.

Under the Spreading Chestnut Tree

Pamela Helberg

February 2010

They say that smell is the sense most likely to evoke strong memories in us. I certainly felt that the day I walked back into my longtime therapist's office for the first time in five years. Walking through the arched brick doorway, through the wrought-iron gate, evoked some familiar feelings in me, but the smells—food from the restaurant below, the collective aroma of serious emotional work, the stench of fear, the crisp freshness of hopes and dreams—all combined to catapult me right back to the chaos of my life eighteen years ago. The pain reached across the years and stabbed at my heart as I climbed the single flight of stairs and listened to the familiar sound of the screen door slamming behind me. I stood still in the foyer for a moment, awash with nostalgia, and looked around. Not much had changed in the waiting room since the first time I sat here: I lowered myself into the chair directly facing the office that belonged to Kate Stout, PhD, Licensed Clinical Psychologist. I sat next to the table with a rotating selection of magazines. I picked up an old *New Yorker* and flipped through the pages. Occasionally, on previous visits, I had taken an issue of the magazine into Kate's office in order to share a cartoon, to give us a laugh and common ground before our session started.

Kate's office rests in the embrace of an ancient chestnut tree twined year-round with white lights, marking the seasons of my visits: bare lighted branches in the winter, golden leaves with the constant plinking of ripened chestnuts, unmoored by the autumn winds, falling to the cobblestones below. The new verdant leaves of spring and summer. When I was a child, we had a chestnut tree in our yard, and the prickly outer shells always fascinated me as it was such a contrast to the soft fuzz inside. I found the bitter unroasted fruit bewildering and utterly inedible. Sitting in Kate's office all these years later, I felt like I had navigated a tightrope that bound me to my childhood, a rope strung from that chestnut tree to this one.

I put down the magazine, closed my eyes, and leaned my head back so it rested against the soothing light blue wall as I waited for the thick, soundproofed door to swing open. I thought about how I had carried so many burdens up those steps and into this room over the years. Sometimes I felt like I might burst before Kate finally appeared at the top of the hour to invite me in. I considered all that had passed, not just since I'd last been to see her, but all that she had seen me through since that initial visit in 1992. The ways in which she had sustained me, buoyed me, listened to me. Empowered me. Helped me find my own sense of agency. I thought everything about me was wrong, flawed, defective somehow. Kate taught me otherwise. From her I learned how to be human, how to begin to ask for help, that I was not nearly as broken as I once believed. I learned to trust myself in the years I saw Kate because she saw me and she did not turn away. Didn't flinch. Or at least, did not let me see it if she did.

The first time I walked into this waiting room with its bland floral art hanging on the walls and seasonally appropriate flower arrangement sitting on the utilitarian side table, I had no idea what to expect from therapy. I was a twenty-nine-year-old adoptive mother of a biracial two-year-old. I had only recently found my way out of religious fundamentalism and the ghosts from that time continued to stalk me. Somehow, I found myself in a long-term lesbian relationship with a much older woman just months after I'd finished a master's degree in English. I settled down without much thought to what I wanted to do with my life. I felt as if I could see life but I couldn't touch life—it was all happening at the far end of a tunnel and I could not reach it. A friend, a psych nurse, gave me Kate's number and encouraged me to make that first call for an appointment.

I arrived in Kate's office with a general sense of unease, uncomfortable in my own skin, uncertain of my role, no clear idea of who I was or what I wanted to be. Who was I to parent a child, let alone a child of color? How was I supposed to respond when random people approached me with comments like, "Wow, is that your baby? Your husband must be very dark." Or, "Is that your baby? Can I touch her hair?" And, my favorite as an adoptive mother, "You sure are fit, you don't look like you just had a baby!" I wasn't even yet thirty. I still felt the weight of my parents' expectations, their implicit disapproval of my life choices thus far. These were the questions I brought to Kate's office initially. These were the weights in my baggage the first time I climbed those stairs.

Life felt gray, I explained. Like I am behind a gauze curtain and can't quite touch nor clearly see what is happening beyond. "I've felt like this my whole life," I stated. "More often than not."

"It sounds to me like you're depressed," Kate said. She crossed her ankles and scribbled on her notepad. She started me on antidepressants then. A new "miracle" drug had recently hit the market, Prozac. I remembered the first time I held that little bit of hope disguised as a green and white capsule, unsure I could wait the four to six weeks Kate said it would take to begin working, transforming me. The pills helped. They lifted the curtain and a million little irritations vanished, the world became a softer, safer place for me to inhabit myself.

I came up those stairs a couple of years later with another secret, and this time I almost quit therapy before I gathered the courage to tell Kate, via a letter in the mail, that I had a compulsion I couldn't seem to control.

"I pull my hair out," I confessed during the appointment I'd made after receiving a letter back from her. I gazed at the carpet, studying my shoes. "I feel around on one spot on my head, find the kinkiest, most wiry piece of hair, and yank it out. Sometimes, I have a bald spot right here the size of a quarter." I placed my right index finger at the crown of my head. I could feel the smooth, hairless patch of scalp beneath my fingertips and resisted an overwhelming urge to scratch. I searched for words that would adequately describe the rush of relief I felt when I pulled out a thick kinky hair. I needed to stop before I had noticeable bald spots. I needed to stop because pulling the hairs made me nauseous, and my fingertips were losing their sense of touch, getting callouses. Besides, it was weird. I felt like a freak.

Kate reached behind her chair into the beige filing cabinet, shuffled through a few folders and turned back around to face me, a photocopied article in her extended hand. I took the article.

"Trich-oh-till-oh-mania," I read. What I had was common enough to have a name. Maybe I wasn't a freak after all.

"Just notice when you have the urge to pull," Kate said. "What's going on when you have that feeling? Write it down. Wear mittens. You can't pull single hairs out, you can't feel them, if you have on mittens."

I don't pull my hair out anymore. My fingers flutter to my head—no bald spots, no smooth patches, nothing interesting. Amazing what comes of paying attention.

And then came the divorce. By then my partner and I had adopted two little girls, and we were ten years into a difficult relationship. Kate saw me hit bottom, watched me struggle, first to make my relationship work and later to stand up for myself, to make the wrenching and necessary decisions to save myself. She continued seeing me even when I was so poor I could not afford to pay her, not even the co-payment. "I'm your therapist," she explained. "Whether you can pay me now or not." She let me haul her yard waste away in my ramshackle old pickup truck in exchange for sessions. She sent me for an alcohol evaluation, stood next to me as I called for credit counseling, teared up when I expressed hopelessness, introduced me to EMDR, came to support me when I had to meet with my ex and our couples counselor. With Kate in the room, I could stay present. Without her, I often felt myself drift away, dissociate, leave my body. I cried in her office, brokenhearted and terrified of losing my girls forever, despondent at being relegated to the every-other-weekend parent.

When I ruminated that perhaps I should just leave town, when I called her in the wee hours of the morning, ready to take a razorblade to my wrists unable to withstand one more day of missing my girls, one more child support payment, one more doubt from anyone that I was in fact, a real parent, Kate reminded me that I did want to see my girls grow up, that I did want to be a steady part of their lives, that even though they could not articulate it, my girls needed me healthy and alive. She reminded me through those dark years that one day, maybe not tomorrow or even next year, but that in fifteen years, twenty years, my children would be grown and we would be a family, still and again.

I opened my eyes and snapped my head forward, realizing those years *had* gone by. I had hung in there, refused to die, refused to go away or let myself be chased out of town. I'd forged new and more creative ways to stay connected to my kids. And here we were! Nearly twenty years later, I had a successful career, my kids were growing up, and by some miracle we were all still in one another's lives. I was on the other side of it all—child support payments? Done. Holiday time disputes? Finished. Joint appearances at school conferences? No more. Independent and healthy relationships with each of my girls? Check! I wanted to run through the soundproof door to Kate's office and shout out "I've *made* it! You were right!" I somehow clawed and scraped my way to the other side and survived. Thrived. All of us had.

* * *

At the top of the hour, Kate's office door opened and a woman I recognized but did not know scurried out, head down, through the waiting room and out the screen door, which banged loudly behind her. Kate appeared and invited me in, looking as she always had: slim, neat, precise. Her thick hair a little grayer now yet still styled in the same short wedge. She had not changed much. I wondered what she saw when she looked at me. Did she see transformation?

Walking into her office, I glanced left, to her desk which was always cluttered, nodded to the chestnut tree outside the window, and took my seat. But it didn't matter. I didn't need Kate anymore. She had given me what I needed years ago, and I had ingested her offering whole. I had done the work, learned the lessons. Now, I simply had to trust my instincts, listen to my gut and go with it.

Pamela Helberg loves writing and therapy in equal measure, as evidenced by her master's degrees in English and Counseling. Pam works as a mental health counselor, and her writing appears in a variety of anthologies. She enjoys running, kayaking, and hanging with her writing buddies. She lives in Bellingham, Washington.

An Incredible Reunion

Peggy Kalpakian Johnson

My mother, Haigouhi Kulakzuzian, was born into an Armenian family in Turkey in 1901. They lived in the city of Adana near the Mediterranean in southenTurkey, and when she was only fourteen years old in 1915, the Turks began their extermination of the Armenian people under the cover of World War I. This is the remarkable story of her survival.

Haigouhi was a day student at the American Congregational Church Seminary for Girls in Adana. (There were no public schools in Adana, certainly not for Armenian girls.) Protestant missionaries had been active in Turkey among the Christian Armenians for decades, especially in education. Haigouhi's family attended the Congregational church in Adana, and she attended their school, where the principal was Miss Grace Towner.

Haigouhi did well in school, where she learned English and French languages, American History, English History, World History, Math, Algebra, and Armenian and Turkish languages. (Only Turkish language was allowed to be spoken publicly in Adana.) Hers was an American education. She must surely have so admired her teachers there, all brave, educated women. (The only other school my mother had been to—prior to attending the Seminary—was Embroidery School.)

Of all her teachers, Grace Towner was to play a major role in Haigouhi's life. That their paths would later cross at all is something of a miracle.

Grace Towner was born in rural Delphos, Kansas, in 1883 and attended Osborne High School and Washburn University in Topeka, Kansas, majoring in English and Literature. After graduation in 1909, now an independent, educated young woman, and against all normal pursuits for young, single women at that time, she left Kansas, took the train to Chicago and enrolled in the Congregational Church Training School, where her classes included Turkish and Armenian languages. At completion, in 1912, she was sent to Adana, Turkey, to begin a forty-year teaching career. Prior to her coming to Adana, education for girls in Turkey was nonexistent. Beginning as a playground director at the Girls' School in Adana, she advanced rapidly and soon became a teacher as well as the Administrator.

Can you imagine how Miss Towner looked to those adolescent Armenian girls? They had never seen a beautiful, young, educated American woman who did not dress like Turkish women, or Armenian women for that matter. Her dress and hairstyles were American. And yet, she could speak her students' language. Those girls loved, admired, adored her. They wanted to be like her.

* * *

Interestingly, about fifteen years after my mother left the Adana School, Miss Towner had a major run-in with the Turkish Government. In April 1931, the Turkish

Government sued Grace Towner, Principal of the Girls' Seminary at Adana, for insulting the Turkish Nationalist Government because she obliged her female students to wear American red-white-and-blue colors. The source said that the trial was covered in worldwide newspapers, but I was unable to locate any details. Presumably, both sides presented their cases. It would be my guess that Miss Towner—fluent in the Turkish language—defended herself. The judge said that he would announce the verdict on April 4, 1931.

Grace Towner stood her ground. Resistant. Still, she persisted. She was acquitted of the charge of insulting the Turkish Government.

Miss Towner served at the Adana Girls' Seminary from 1912 to 1931 when the school was closed. Whether the Turks insisted that it be closed, or if the closure resulted from the worldwide Depression, I do not know, but I am certain Miss Towner was heartbroken. Her life's work had been dedicated to the education of Armenian girls in Adana, and she had seen the school grow in numbers and scholastic standing in her twenty years there.

For one year following, she taught in the Turkish Lycée in Adana. In 1933, she moved to the Tarsus American College for Women where she taught English and English literature and served as Associate Principal. In 1946, she moved to the Uskudar American Academy for Girls, where she taught the same subjects and also was an administrator.

At nearly seventy years of age, in 1952, Miss Towner finally left Turkey and retired to a missionary retirement home. She lived out her days there, dying in 1968 at the age of eighty-five. Grace Towner was honored as one of the early educators of female students in Turkey. Missionaries, colleagues, and students honored her for her service, for her faith, for her dedication to her students, and to education for women. She was an inspiration to many.

* * *

Miss Towner did more than inspire. She also saved lives. One day in 1915 at the height of Turkish extermination of the Armenian people, Grace Towner came to the home of her student, Haigouhi Kulakzuzian and asked her mother if she would permit Haigouhi to move into the school as a live-in student. In 1915, the Americans had not yet entered World War I, and Miss Towner would have known the American school was a safe place. Perhaps the only safe place.

My guess is that Miss Towner probably invited all of her Armenian students to do the same, to shelter under the American roof. Miss Towner told Haigouhi's mother that Haigouhi could work and teach in the school for her room and board. Haigouhi's mother agreed that her daughter could go live at the school.

On the roof of the school, Miss Towner had students spread out a large American flag and fasten it down. Any combatants flying over the city would know this was an American domain.

To pay her way, Haigouhi waited on tables and made the teachers' beds. She graduated from the Adana Girls' Seminary on April 11, 1917 in a class of ten young women. In the graduation photograph she is the only one smiling. She continued living at the school after graduation, doing some teaching as well.

When she parted with her mother, father, and little brother Haigaz, did Haigouhi suspect she would never see them again? If so, she never said so to me. Shortly after she moved into the American school, her family were all rounded up and marched into the desert where her father died of starvation and her mother was killed. Her little brother ran away into the desert.

* * *

While Haigouhi was a student, her aunt, who worked in a factory where they made canvas for the Turkish war effort, wanted her to meet the single, handsome, young Armenian foreman. She invited Haigouhi, the young man, his mother, and sister to her home for an afternoon visit. This was a custom typical of arranged marriages at that time. Nearly all marriages were arranged, especially in wartime when there were so few men.

Haigouhi's aunt told her, "After they say hello, you make some Turkish coffee—and serve it. If his mother says, 'This is good coffee,' they like you, and the wedding plans can go forward."

The young man's mother did compliment Haigouhi's coffee.

But when her aunt asked Haigouhi about the prospective husband, the girl had one question: "Can he read and write?" The answer was no. At that, Haigouhi said, "Forget it! To read and write is very important to me."

As a student and a young teacher, Haigouhi and her classmates often visited a dry goods shop where a handsome young clerk, Haroutune Kalpakian, worked. No doubt she and Haroutune carried on a flirtation that led to his asking Miss Towner for permission to marry Haigouhi. Despite the fact that his religion was Armenian Apostolic, Miss Towner agreed—the times were too uncertain to insist on a Protestant husband for her young student. I'm sure Haigouhi's parting with Miss Towner was very emotional and sad.

Armenians in that turbulent era could not gather in public places, not even in a church, perhaps especially not in a church. So, an Armenian Apostolic priest came to Haroutune's family's apartment to perform the marriage on October 18, 1917.

* * *

A few years later in 1923, Haigouhi, Haroutune, and their two little daughters—including me, a toddler—emigrated to Los Angeles where Haigouhi's older brother and sister had emigrated years before. Here, the Kalpakians had two more daughters; they worked hard and made good lives for themselves. They became proud American citizens.

Fast-forward now too many years later—1953—in Los Angeles.

My sister's husband, Finley Bown, saw a notice in their Congregational Church newsletter that Miss Grace Towner, a missionary teacher, had retired to Los Angeles from Turkey. She was living in a Congregational retirement home. Since everyone in our family knew the story, Finley recognized Grace Towner's name, and alerted Mama.

Mama drove to the retirement home, taking her youngest daughter, Harriett, then age seventeen, with her. They went to Miss Towner's room.

When Miss Towner looked up and saw Harriett, she said, "Haigouhi?"

Harriett at seventeen looked so much like the youthful Haigouhi that the years seemed to roll away. What a joyous reunion!

Mama invited Miss Towner to come to our house on West Olympic Boulevard for a Sunday afternoon visit. Miss Towner got to meet Haroutune Kalpakian again, thirty-six years after she had agreed to the marriage. In the dining room of my parents' lovely home, Mama served lunch to Miss Towner, Armenian food she made with her own hands. I feel certain that she made coffee in the correct way as well.

Mama arranged for each of her four daughters to come that afternoon with our husbands and children to meet Miss Towner. Because there were so many of us and so many little children, and she was so elderly, we visited with her one family at a time. My daughter, Laura, who was eight years old at the time, remembers meeting Miss Towner at her grandmother's house that Reunion Sunday. We were all honored to have met Miss Towner in person, and thanked her for saving Mama's life. Then we went outside and took pictures in the sunshine.

In the midst of this happy, almost unbelievable reunion, I could not help wondering if Miss Towner had flashback memories to World War I in Adana, Turkey, and the American school sheltering Armenian children from the Turks. I wondered if she remembered the departure of her sixteen-year-old student to whom she had granted permission to marry Haroutune Kalpakian. I feel certain this 1953 reunion was the answer to Miss Towner's parting prayer for Haigouhi in 1917.

I would like to add here my own twenty-first-century tribute to Miss Grace Towner—a courageous young woman who left her safe American home in the early years of the twentieth century, learned Turkish and Armenian languages, and traveled to Turkey to teach young Armenian girls in an American Christian school. As an American citizen, she stood up to the Turkish Army during World War I. I know her students adored her. I adored her. She saved her students' lives and I am honored that I was able to meet her, in person, at that 1953 reunion.

Thank you for your courage and love, Grace Towner.

Peggy Kalpakian Johnson was born in Constantinople in 1922. As a toddler, she emigrated with her family to Los Angeles where they—and she—became proud American citizens. She is mother to four children, grandmother to two grandsons, and great-grandmother to two girls. "An Incredible Reunion" is her third publication.

Poetry: Accidental and Occasional

Linda Q. Lambert

I worshipped Mr. Agol, my high-school English teacher, a big man with an easy laugh, poor posture, Coke-bottle glasses, and a passion for teaching. One scorching afternoon in our un-air-conditioned classroom at Mt. Whitney High School in Visalia, California, he stood in front of the class and belted out the first line of Felicia Dorothea Hemans' poem "Casablanca": "The *boy* stood *on* the *burn*ing *deck.*"

"That's iambic!" he continued. "Say it with me." We repeated the words, overemphasizing the appropriate syllables as instructed. "Iambic," he continued, "is the main rhythm for poems in English.

"If you write poetry—and some of you might—tell the truth, be believable. There's a word for that: *verisimilitude.* If you think good fences make good neighbors, like Frost, say so."

I hadn't thought about writing poetry, although that year, my junior year, I fancied the lyricism of Whitman, which, no doubt, crept into my essay on trees. Mr. Agol scrawled across the top of page one, *Pure poetry, but your handwriting is atrocious.* I flipped the paper over to see my grade: A+ for content; F for penmanship and grammar. Getting an F was overshadowed by the notion of being an accidental poet—the moment when the possibility of writing poetry lodged itself into my adolescent consciousness.

I was one of the editors of *Scribblathology,* a slim mimeographed anthology produced by Scribblers, the creative writing club. We dedicated it to our faculty adviser. When Mr. Agol, the relentless evaluator of our weekly themes, discovered two typos on the dedication page, he laughed, applauding our overall effort instead of discrediting a flawed publication.

Once, having listened to the chatter of me and two of my Scribblers friends, he described us as "delightfully fey." I didn't know what "fey" meant, but delivered as it was with one of his whole-body laughs, I figured the word was complimentary.

He remains, for me, the gold standard in teachers.

* * *

I entered the University of Southern California as a journalism major, switched to English literature, then considered changing again when I received the following comment on my *Il Penseroso* (Milton) paper: *You will receive an F if you do not redo this paper and explicate this poem. Be specific.* Chilling words for an English major.

I decided to rewrite and was toiling over the revision at Doheny Library when a graduate student I knew slightly asked what I was working on.

"Oh," she said. "I know that poem."

"I was afraid to ask what 'explicate' meant. I looked it up. I still don't understand."

"Explication just means looking at the structure and the rhyme scheme and the imagery. Let's go through it. I'll help you." By the time the library closed, I had a rough draft.

"Do you need a ride somewhere?" she asked. I said yes, even though my dorm was close.

We sat in front of College Hall, enclosed in the darkness of her Volkswagen bug. Did I know the poems of Theodore Roethke? No. She'd taken a class from Roethke at the University of Washington. Then she switched on the light, reached into the backseat for a book, and began reading. "I knew a woman, lovely in her bones / When small birds sighed, she would sigh back at them."

"Isn't that romantic?" she said. Yes, I thought, and I feel romantic about you. But I didn't say that, nor did I foresee how that feeling might play out in my life. Despite the intimacy of sitting together, I had the sense that she was simply sharing her deep love of poetry. That night, she was my teacher.

I did not see her again, but her enthusiasm for her Roethke drove me to read more of his work.

* * *

I continued in English, taking Modern British Literature from a newly minted PhD from the University of Washington. On the first day of class, Dr. Kennett Moritz sat on the floor until someone determined that the guy in the khakis and the loosely knotted tie was the professor. He arose, a winsome smile upon his face, introduced himself, and asked us our names. He read poetry with rousing passion, sounding like a beckoning, street-corner poet-evangelist. No singsong burning-deck fervor, but bold renderings of "Do Not Go Gentle Into That Good Night" and "The Force That Through the Green Fuse Drives the Flower."

The World's Fair was held in Seattle in 1962. My parents wanted to go and—always supportive of my education—were willing to pay for summer session at UW. I read Dr. Moritz's dissertation, "Visual Organization in Dickens," stumbling through the unfamiliar territory of scholarly work in the quiet of Suzallo Library. I was sad to discover that Roethke was not on campus that summer.

* * *

After obtaining a BA in English, I hitchhiked through Great Britain, making my way to Laugharne, South Wales where Dylan Thomas had lived. A bartender at the Browns Hotel, which had a small shelf of Thomas books, sold me *A Child's Christmas in Wales* and gave me directions to the Boat House where the Thomases had lived. I hopped over the fence, and peered through the windows of the place he called his "word splashed hut"—a spare space with a simple desk, a colorless rug, and a scattering of books. I felt enveloped in reverence, sitting near The Boat House, enchanted that I was reading Dylan Thomas' poetry right there. I didn't stay long. I was a trespasser; someone could kick me off the property.

Three days later, I sat at a pub in Rye, the town where Henry James lived, and cobbled together enough material on my experience in Laugharne to merit publication in a literary magazine called *The Laurel Review*.

After returning from Europe, I published my very first poem in *Statement*, Cal State LA's literary magazine. "The Odd Hot" was a strange little offering comparing the pounding touch required for a manual typewriter to the light strokes and heat of an electric IBM. The editor called to tell me of the poem's acceptance: "I want to know that in ten years you are still writing poetry."

Ten years later I *was* writing—bits of doggerel to entertain, persuade, or distract my children. To eradicate my eight-year-old daughter's bad habit, I composed a rhyme she grew to hate: "Extract your digit from your oral cavity; sucking your thumb's not good for you or me."

Once, at a series of stoplights, to squelch the backseat squabbles of three preschoolers, I concocted:

> ABC Up in a tree / DEF There's a chef / GHI Say
> Hi / JKLM His name is Clem /
> NOP Stung by a bee / QRS What a mess / TUV
> Oh, don't you see / WXYZ Never cook in a tree /
> Never cook in a tree / Never cook in a tree.

"Stung by a Bee's" durability exists not in publication, but in its repetition by grandchildren in the twenty-first century. During those child-raising years, I read the *Selected Poems of Gabriela Mistral*, which captured maternity for me. I am convinced that the rapture of a few lines of poetry offset interrupted sleep, colicky babies, and the drastic rearrangement of routines that accompany the entrance of children into family life.

In 1997, I earned an MLS and secured a job as a community college library director. The library's marketing committee created *The Kumquat Challenge*, an annual contest in which participants composed poems that included seven predetermined words. I submitted a poem every year, including a haiku—prodded by a friend.

"I don't know anything about Haiku, and I don't like fixed patterns."

"Just try," she said. "If you don't like it, quit."

I liked it. I got into the five-seven-five rhythm. By marrying my anxiety about haiku with research about Matsuo Basho (1644-1694), a Japanese samurai who abandoned his status to devote himself to poetry, I came up with "Haiku, How Do I Write You?"

> Five seven then five
> haiku how do I write you?
> Come syllables come.

> Key for poets now
> Basho: sixteen sixty two,
> his first verse birthed.

> Who will carry poems
> light as Basho's hiking bag
> bursting with quick truth?

After retirement, I signed up for Introduction to Poetry at Whatcom Community College. Dr. Ron Leatherbarrow walked into class and gave us some ground rules:

"I'm obsessive about being on time. Try not to be late."

"Be prepared for flash quizzes. Make sure you read the material."

"I'm sorry that our text *Sound & Sense* now costs $125 instead of the $8 when I first used it the fall of 1965 . . . now . . . tell me what you think poetry is."

When a student asked if we could spend class time on our own poetry, he said, "Sure. Nobody has asked to do that in my fifty years of teaching." He listened to each poem, remarking about specific components he liked, making suggestions for revision.

Unlike Dr. Moritz's reading of "Do Not Go Gentle Into That Good Night," Dr. Leatherbarrow's recitation of "Do Not Go Gentle . . ." was cadenced and slow, his voice solemn. He acknowledged that he and his father "had a complicated and difficult relationship," and that he'd presented this poem at his funeral.

Class members and friends of Dr. Leatherbarrow's were invited to "The Last Word," an open mic at a downtown pub celebrating the professor's retirement, so I wrote an occasional poem:

Wiseguy with Gravitas

The teacher strides into English 113.
His leather hat tilted, his beard trimmed,
his jeans pressed. He has stature and gravitas,
a contrast to the dash and dishabille
of the sweatshirt-clad student
coiled into a corner chair.

Teaching poetry since 1965,
is his much-loved night job.
He listens to our poetry.
He makes jokes, refers to himself
as a wiseguy. Then:
"Now that we've had fun, he says,

"Take out a sheet of paper,"
the dreaded words announcing a quiz.
    What is a trochee?
    What does Keats say about autumn?
    What color is the moth in Frost's "Design"?

Should scansion occur
of this man's time upon the planet,
irregularities are likely to exist.
Our biographies,
however steady our hands
upon the pages of our days,
do not conform to a fixed form,
a villanelle, a sestina, a sonnet.

He is living the life he wanted to live,
teaching students who want to learn
so that we too can have
rhythm in our steps,
similes in our statements,
and wisdom in our stories.

My poetry writing goals are modest, interwoven with creative nonfiction and memoir. Billy Collins says that moving from title to first line is like "stepping into a canoe." I'll step into the canoe of poetry and fall into the water a few times by forgetting to wear the life jacket of free verse, straitjacketed and challenged instead by unfamiliar forms with names like ekphrastic and ruba'i.

I'll write for *The Kumquat Challenge* and create a poem a day for Paul Nelson's August Postcard Fest. I'll attend monthly Poetry Club meetings, a small-group outgrowth of English 113. I'll shower syllables of a rhyming nature upon my grandchildren, aided by Clement Wood's *The Complete Rhyming Dictionary,* a book I've consulted since the date marked on the inside page: 1982. One never knows when there'll be a chance to rhyme "bouquet" with "Bordelais" or "archpriest" with "artiste."

I seek to be worthy of Mr. Agol's description—fey, in the sense of whimsical and magical. On an occasional basis.

Linda Q. Lambert published an article at sixteen, a poem and essay at twenty-six, a guidebook at thirty-one. Aside from an article about childbirth in a Volkswagen, she replaced literary productivity with raising seven children, a library career, and completion of an MFA. In progress: Untold (memoir), poetry, creative nonfiction.

The Finger

Richard N. Little

The Washington State ferry made its ponderous way through the fog. Standing on the foredeck, we peered ahead, chilly in windbreakers and scarves. Passage between murky islands and past sudden rocks seemed fraught to us despite the undoubted skill of the boat's captain. What good would periodic blasts of a deafening horn do if some small craft got in the way? A pair of seagulls hovered above the bow, then disappeared into the thick mist. Our jackets glistened with the wet, and the cold breeze of the boat's movement sent us back into the nearly empty passenger compartment. This wasn't starting out as the sunny escape to the San Juan Islands we had in mind.

Lopez Island, to be specific.

As with many a longtime couples, our spousal twosome needed this getaway. Our traditional patience with each other had been fraying. Some days, even my "good mornings" sounded snarky. "Want more coffee?" from my wife often sounded to me like a threat. Why not escape to an island? *Isola* in Latin; as in, isolate for a while. Let others back home deal with impatient drivers, frustrated grocery clerks, unhappy clients, unhelpful coworkers, ugly scandal, thankless deadlines, and rude passersby. We would forswear the newspaper and its daily reminder of the national pall and read mindless paperbacks instead. No TV, no e-mail, no wireless, period.

* * *

The San Juan Islands consist of four hundred islands (more or less, depending on the height of the tide) most of which are uninhabited and unnamed. They make up a gorgeous archipelago that lies in the Salish Sea between Washington State and Vancouver Island, British Columbia. The scenery is the stuff of calendar covers, postcards, and professional photographs throughout the Northwest. Granite scarps rise out of the sea. Evergreens, oaks, and madrona trees climb down hillsides all the way to the water, the color of which ranges from slate to cobalt, depending on the day. Or the polished green of a bottle shard you find washed up on the beach. On the best days, a miracle of dark, shimmering blue happens that mirrors the clearest sky in the US. There are whales, too, including the iconic orcas.

Four of the San Juans are accessible by the state ferry system. Each of them is beautiful in its own way and has its own personality. Eponymous San Juan is the most populous. It boasts the picturesque town of Friday Harbor, the county seat. Despite summer crowds on busy streets and sidewalks, a pedestrian will look in vain for a stoplight.

Orcas Island, larger by two square miles, considers itself a bit artier. It caters to folks who want to avoid tourists but who nonetheless don't mind frequenting fairly upscale shops and restaurants that only a healthy tourist trade can sustain.

Shaw Island, population 240, is unique, too. For many years, ferry passengers were charmed upon arrival by watching nuns (Franciscan Sisters of the Eucharist) wearing bright reflective safety vests over their brown habits, "manning" the dock–hauling ropes, lowering the off-ramp, and directing cars onto the island. No longer do they perform these tasks, nor do they run the deli and store that is located at the landing. In 2004, the three remaining sisters sadly decided it was time to move on.

Our goal, Lopez, is relatively flat, a favorite of cyclists, and not terribly crowded. The only commercial center, Lopez Village, consists of two markets, a bakery, a couple of real estate offices, a few assorted shops, a community center, the obligatory coffee boutique, a handful of restaurants, and a quite lovely book shop. That's about it. There's a church here or there on the island, a library, a motel, a school, and not much else.

When we approached the dock, as if on cue the fog broke and disappeared. Puffy white clouds replaced it, and like something out of a seagoing adventure movie, bright sunlight glared off our big green-and-white boat and danced along the water. We drove up the ramp, following the vehicle in front of us in a slow procession that gradually picked up speed. It was fall, and with our windows down, the island air was glorious. There could be nothing amiss in this idyllic space. Our moods improved. We longed for peace and quiet. What never entered our minds, however, was a certain clubbiness on the part of year-round residents we encountered. The ratio of tourists to natives on Lopez is low, to be sure, but still. Why were we given . . . The Finger?

* * *

On our way to Lopez Village, only five miles distant, the driver of an oncoming car flipped us a finger—or so it seemed. Curious, but we both pretended not to notice and didn't give it a second thought. In town, there were groceries to buy before setting off again to the house we'd rented for a three-day weekend.

After shopping and getting back on our way, the rudeness happened again. It sure looked like the guy behind the wheel of another car flipped us off. There were few other cars on the road and bicycles had thinned out. The beauty all around us might present a safety challenge, but my driving was fine. What was this finger thing about?

"Honey, did you see that?" said my spouse. "Was he waving at us?"

"Some wave," I said.

Another car passed and the woman driving smiled, digits raised in our direction. Ever the glass-full kind of guy, I said "There's something we're missing."

"Jeez, should we reciprocate?"

"Uh sure. I'll do it. See what happens." As the next car approached, I raised my hand off the steering wheel and lifted a finger. "There! I did it."

My wife figured it out. "Hon, you did it wrong."

"What do you mean?"

"Wrong finger! It's supposed to be a greeting, I think. So use a different finger."

"You're right. Here, I'll try with this guy."

A baseball-capped codger driving a faded blue pickup passed us.

"How'd I do?"

"Better, dear. But your technique needs work."

We encountered no other cars, or maybe we didn't notice. As any visitor will report, the drop-dead scenery is overwhelming. We pulled over to catch our breath and take it all in. There was a brief shower after which sun streaks lit up the brilliant yellows and reds of trees. Hundreds of droplets hung from salmonberry bushes like drops of fire, and cabbage rose hips glistened like Christmas tree garlands strung along weathered cedar fence lines.

A solitary wren chirped and dashed for cover. Two hares, one dun-colored, the other black, scampered through the grass beside us and disappeared. As if on cue, a golden eagle passed overhead. Back on the road, we passed emerald-green fields with horses and cattle and llamas. There were clusters of sea birds foraging inland: hungry ravens, flocks of robins, busy juncos, and noisy crows everywhere. We were careful to watch for deer. A twenty-minute drive to our abode took an hour.

We did what we'd promised ourselves we'd do. We slept. We took walks. We read on a porch that had a peek-a-boo view of a small bay. We reconnected, and *connected* to our precious lives, as Mary Oliver advises, making the effort to pay attention on strolls through the fields.

And it worked. Each day, sparkles of sunlight would break through mid-morning fog. We called them beacons of the lives we were thankful to have. We asked ourselves how we might do things better back on the mainland, and we wondered how Lopez islanders fared.

Did we find out? A bit. Across much of the island, tree-lined driveways led to secluded homes. Solitude, or isolation?

The last day, we packed up and set off back to the ferry landing. Toward us came a car. There it was again. I'd forgotten the lesson of the earlier drive. Oops. It was going to take more than a couple of trips on the island to get it and feel like part of the tribe. The locals surely noticed my feeble, amateurish attempts along the finger-wave learning curve because I'm positive we saw some barely suppressed grins.

But then success!

Want the secret for mastering the genuine Lopez Island greeting, guaranteed to erase the word mainlander stenciled across the front of your car?

Don't lift your hand from the wheel at all. And don't use just the index finger. The absolute sexiest is the first two fingers of the left hand, just slightly apart, and raised no more than three inches off the steering wheel. Hold it for barely one count. Simple.

The aha moment? When you know you've got it?

My wife shook her head disapprovingly at an approaching car. "Honey, did you see that?"

"Yeah. She waved her whole hand."

"Damn tourist!"

* * *

It's working though, you know, that trick we learned on "The Friendly Isle"—Lopez Island's nickname, we later learned. A lot depends on paying attention.

I can still come downstairs grumpy in the morning. My wife, whose role in our family is to stay informed about current events, can still grumble aloud about the latest idiocy in the news. But, often as not, she'll glance over at me and, one hand still holding the paper, raise two digits and give me the fingers, plural.

Richard Little, retired attorney and lobbyist, has been published in the Seattle Times, Seattle Post-Intelligencer, The Santa Fe Writers Project, Cirque, *and* Clover, a Literary Rag. *Dick's story collections, Postcards from the* Road *and* Jakey's Fork *will soon be joined by a novel, City Haul. Read his blog at Pepys2000.blogspot.com*

An Indian Picnic

Debu Majumdar

One Saturday afternoon, we four friends weren't doing anything particular. We sat in the small neighborhood park, eating peanuts with green *tetul* chutney and longed very much to do something extraordinary. We were about fifteen years old then. Debjit said we could go to his uncle's second house in Barasat, twenty miles away. That caught our fancy.

"We can go for a picnic," I said.

"I always wanted to cook chicken." Shibu's face lit up in anticipation.

"We haven't done this before; it would be great fun," Bikash said, clapping his hands.

"My aunt would be mad," Debjit said in an alarmed voice, "if she knew we cooked chicken in her kitchen." His face became pensive. He was the first among us to develop a distinct mustache. That made him look more somber.

We never ate chicken in our home; we ate fish, goat meat, sometimes lamb, but never chicken. It wasn't forbidden by our religion, but Muslims raised chickens, so Hindus wouldn't eat chicken or let chickens near their house. I wanted to do it, but my mind vacillated, *so much depends upon my family not finding out.* Since I was usually the most cautious in our group, I added, "But no one should know about it, especially my family and Debjit's aunt."

"You said they are in town and rarely go to Barasat. How would she know?" Bikash asked Debjit assertively.

Shibu promised Debjit that we would clean up the place so completely, no one would know we had been there.

"I'll be in big trouble," Debjit said weakly, "if my aunt even suspects it. She may not let me enter their house ever again."

"Don't worry," Shibu assured him, "there won't be a trace of chicken anywhere."

* * *

Debjit's uncle gave him the key without hesitation. He was happy that we would check on the empty house. "My uncle said he would have joined us, but he has a meeting to organize the local *Durga puja.*" He chuckled, and we were relieved. Our plan remained intact.

We started very early in the morning. The train journey was wonderful because few people traveled on Sundays and we found empty seats. As the train chugged along, soon densely packed houses gave way to the green scenery of villages. I loved looking at banana trees behind the huts and green rice fields waving in the wind. Shibu and Bikash sang Tagore songs. Debjit played drums on the wooden seat. Time passed quickly and we reached Barasat station.

We went straight to the market nearby. The market looked chaotic with vendors on both sides of the narrow road and shoppers all around. Fish and goat meat were sold inside a tin shed; a fishy smell surrounded the area. No chicken meat sold anywhere.

We finally found live chickens at the end of the market. Two sellers kept them in round cane baskets—about a foot high and four feet in diameter—with a loose, beige net on top. The thin, middle-aged men had unkempt goatees, and wore checkered *lungi* that we associated with Muslim men. We hesitated for several seconds and quickly diverted our gaze to the chickens. They were of many different sizes and colors. Their round eyes appeared alert, and they moved their heads constantly to look around.

"After coming this far, we cannot give up now," Shibu said. "We can cut chickens."

We bought two of the biggest chickens—one mottled yellow and brown, one dark red. The seller tied the chickens' legs with a cord to carry them, legs up. We walked along in the direction of the house. We saw a sweet store and bought the best sweets they had.

Debjit slowed down when he saw a well-kept restaurant, *Mughlai Khana*. "Why don't we buy *mutton kababs* for tea?"

Shibu glanced at the restaurant skeptically. "Are you sure they aren't beef kababs?"

"It's a restaurant in Barasat," Debjit said. "They wouldn't dare." He walked straight into the restaurant and bought the kababs. We were in a good mood and excited because whatever we did felt like we were crossing a line we weren't supposed to. We were also cheerful because Shibu, our great cook, was with us. Once he cooked goat meat—so wonderful we never forgot it. We looked forward to his cooking.

When we reached the house, the sun was already high, but we were in no hurry. The one-story stucco house looked big. We entered through the main door and opened all the windows to remove the musty smell. The red cement floors of the drawing room and the kitchen felt cool and pleasant. After we examined the rooms and the kitchen, we went to the backyard. The large, walled garden had several trees, and the grass hadn't been cut for some time, but we didn't care.

Shibu brought out the chickens and left them just outside the door, plainly in our view. Bikash took out the badminton rackets, and Debjit and I rushed to select our rackets immediately. It was clear, everyone wanted to delay the killing.

We played badminton for a while. But when we couldn't postpone any longer, I found no one wanted to do the job. Debjit and Bikash claimed, "I don't know how."

"Cowards," I told them in an annoyed voice. "Give me a big knife, I'll show you."

Debjit brought the chickens to the middle of the backyard; immediately, they started to squawk and thrash about violently.

Bikash held down the red chicken and ordered me, "Don't take too long."

"As if you know what to do!" I shot back. I held the head and started to cut the neck, but the knife was not sharp enough, and my hand trembled. The chicken moved frantically. My heart beat fast. I became nervous; I felt I couldn't do the job, but then Debjit, who was standing next to me, shouted, "Press hard." I closed my eyes and did what he said. Blood squirted out, and Bikash let go of the chicken; it flew twenty feet while I had its little head in my hand—red, wet, and slippery. More blood came out of its body throbbing on the green grass. It was unbelievable. I felt bad and exhausted, and couldn't cut the second chicken. Shibu had to do it.

Plucking feathers was another job. We didn't know how, so it took a long time; chicken feathers flew all over the backyard. After the feathers were plucked, we all agreed, we must have tea now.

"And kababs," Debjit added.

* * *

Shibu gutted and cut the chickens in the kitchen. We admired his zeal. He was a little heavier set than us, and with his shirt off, long black hair, and heavy eyebrows, he looked like the chefs who cook at weddings; we felt he was perfect for the job. I stood near him, ready to help, but really to watch. Debjit sipped tea and furtively glanced around as if to see if any other person was there. Only Bikash got involved with Shibu, handing him utensils and spices. Bikash was the smallest among us, but he was quick on his feet and of great help.

Shibu first sautéed onions with fresh ginger, garlic, and whole red chilies; then he put in the chicken pieces and fried them. He added turmeric and a little cumin and coriander powder, and kept on stirring the pieces. He put cinnamon sticks, whole cardamoms, and a few cloves, and when the chicken pieces turned brown, he filled the pot with water to boil the meat. A spicy aroma filled the room.

We stood around, chatting and waiting for the meat to be cooked. Shibu was happy to remain busy; he started rice and cleaned the stove area. We expected the dish to take a long time to cook as it takes for goat meat, but the meat was done quickly. We hoped for a dry, spicy chicken curry, but to our astonishment the water in the pot didn't reduce much. It seemed more water had come out of the chicken and the dish became a soup—a yellow broth with chunks of white meat. Not appetizing at all.

Shibu sighed and admitted, "I guess you don't cook chicken like goat meat."

We ate a little of his chicken with rice, and found it pretty bad. The meat was tasteless, and we couldn't mix rice with the watery gravy—the way we like to eat.

We relished the store-bought sweets and went out to play in the backyard. That was more fun.

Debjit suggested we should clean the backyard first, but we ignored him and started to play badminton again. The sun slid down the sky, but we kept on playing.

Then we heard a knock at the door. Who would come to visit now? We all rushed to the front door and saw Debjit's uncle standing there. He was a short, stout man with a round face. It was unexpected; we couldn't speak for a few seconds, and just stood there in front of him.

He broke the impasse. "Ah! How do you like the place?"

Debjit quickly pulled him inside the house, while the rest of us ran to the garden to collect chicken feathers. But we weren't fast enough; his uncle saw us and came out.

Debjit's uncle looked around, surveying the mess in the yard. "Where did the chicken feathers come from?"

We didn't answer him and kept on picking up the feathers.

"Hmmm, you boys cooked chicken?" He turned to Debjit, "You know what your aunt would do?" His angry voice sent a shiver down our spines.

Debjit avoided his eyes and meekly said, "They wanted to try out a new dish."

"I don't know what to tell your aunt," he told Debjit. "She wants to spend some time here next week, so I came to fix a few things." He stooped down to see how tall the grass was. He then turned toward us. "You fellows clean up the backyard. I don't want to see a trace of chicken here."

Bikash was quick to respond. "We'll remove all the feathers; no one will ever know a chicken was here."

The uncle's voice softened slightly. "I've never had home-cooked chicken, how does it taste?"

"It doesn't taste good," we all told him almost in unison.

He went inside. Shibu followed him.

Debjit looked disheartened and glum. He started to pick up the feathers as fast as he could, but Bikash and I were slower—we felt so sorry for what might happen to Debjit that we couldn't focus on cleaning up. Bikash collected the feathers near the house, and I went to the farthest part of the garden. I wanted to stay away from Debjit's uncle. We all did. We stayed out as long as we could. Finally, when we couldn't find any more feathers, we went inside.

The three of us stopped short at the door, staring at the scene. Debjit's eyes became large and his mouth fell open. His uncle was sitting comfortably in a chair with a brass plate in his hand, happily eating. Shibu stood at his elbow with the pot of chicken in one hand and a serving spoon in the other. "Quite good," he was telling

Shibu. "You said you put a lot of *garam masala*?" A convivial grin spread over his face.

"Shall I give you a little more?"

"Well," he looked at Shibu, "don't you want to leave some for your friends?" But he stretched out his plate for more.

"No, no," Shibu told him emphatically. "They had plenty. Please finish up what's left in the pot." Shibu gave him all he had.

Debjit's uncle held the plate near his chest, crossed one leg over the other, and continued savoring the chicken curry.

"I've never seen him enjoy a dish so much," Debjit murmured, shocked. He leaned toward me and whispered in my ear, "My aunt is a vegetarian."

Debu Majumdar's novel, Sacred River: A Himalayan Journey, *won first place in the 2016 Chanticleer Somerset contest (adventure/suspense) and was one of three finalists for the 2017 Nancy Pearl award. His other works are:* From the Ganges to the Snake River *(creative nonfiction) and four children's books in the* Viku and the Elephant *series.*

A Snowstorm, a TV, and a Human Connection

Cheryl Stritzel McCarthy

Snow swirls down, thicker and thicker as the wind gusts it into drifts. On this Monday in February in our Pacific Northwest town of Bellingham, school is canceled and many businesses aren't opening.

My husband, Bob, still manages his 5:00 am twenty-two-mile commute north to the refinery where he works. He's worked for the same company for thirty-five years and never missed a day. He's *nice*, the kind of nice that prompts my female friends to wish—aloud, in front of me—that they'd married him.

Bob phones me mid-afternoon. "We need to deliver that TV tonight. Remember I'm flying out tomorrow for a conference, so tonight it is."

"Okaaayyy," I exhale into the phone, but I'm thinking, *What?! You said we would deliver our used fifty-inch TV tonight? Delivery is not our responsibility. That's not the way this works!*

Two weeks before, Bob purchased a new HD-4K, widescreen, super-sharp TV, a beauty with the latest technology. It meant we had to get rid of our previous big screen. Bob posted our five-year-old, works-great model on Craigslist for one hundred dollars and received a call from a guy in Montana. Montana-man wanted to buy it for his sister, who lives in our town. Bob had agreed to *deliver* the giant unwieldy thing to the sister, for no charge of course.

Which required my participation. It would take two of us to even shift the old fifty-incher off its stand in our den. This phone call is the first I'd heard of the arrangement.

"At least wait 'til the check clears." I struggle to keep annoyance out of my voice.

"It cleared," Bob replies.

"Okay, sweetie." Like it or not, I am going to deliver a big-screen TV tonight.

I look out the window. The wind is belting heavy snow into six-inch drifts across our driveway. Freezing sleet is hammering the skylight in the kitchen. The storm is gaining strength, whipping snow horizontally and drumming it against the window.

Bob arrives home at 6:00 pm. His apple-red sedan is covered with icy muck from roof to running board, fender to fender. I kick a boulder-size clump of frozen crud off its rear.

"Where's her phone number?" I say without preamble. "I'm calling to at least make sure she's home."

I let it ring. I'm about to hang up when a voice of indeterminate age answers. "Yeah, I'm here."

She's grouchy? Isn't that my prerogative here? I keep my voice neutral and reply we'll set off soon.

We stand at each end of the big-screen in our den. Awkwardly, searching for handholds, we gingerly lift and maneuver the thing out the door, into the narrow hallway, past the kitchen, and into the garage. Annoyed though I am, I'm worried about Bob. He's fit but has seriously bad knees from decades of basketball and tennis.

Panting a bit, keeping the giant TV vertical, we approach the back of my open-hatch, all-wheel-drive Subaru.

"It doesn't fit." Bob says this as if it's news. *How could you not have measured it ahead of time?* I scream in my head.

"Turn it horizontally." Bob fixes things. He doesn't waste time blaming.

We hoist it carefully over the lip of the hatch. Then I sprint round to the side door and crawl inside. Twisting, torquing my back, I reach toward the edge of the TV. It looks like an aircraft carrier slow-steaming toward me. Awkwardly, I lift its front edge over folded-down backseats.

"It's in!" Bob closes the hatch, we jump into the front seats, and he taps the sister's address into my car's navigation system.

We crawl through neighborhood streets, gray and ghostly in the storm, only a few other headlights piercing the gloom. We swing onto Interstate 5. I've never seen our hometown interstate like this, covered with half a foot of icy slush. At one point, following what looks like the tracks of traffic, we realize we've been driving on the shoulder.

Twenty-five minutes later, we exit into the Birchwood neighborhood, our eyes fixed on the navigation system's bright-lit map. We're on the right street. We drive up and down, turn around in a deep hump of snow, the Subaru's tires spinning. The pin of the sister's address shows on the map. The actual location of the sister remains tantalizing out of reach. The neighborhood is a jumble of houses and parking lots and low-rise apartment buildings, some set behind others in a baffling mix of dwellings lost in the swirling snow.

Bob picks one driveway out of many and turns in. It leads behind a row of houses and opens onto a parking lot that serves half a dozen three-story apartment buildings. "This is it."

I have no idea how he's found it.

Every parking spot is full, each car humped with snow. No one here has left home today. The only spot available is the handicapped one. He backs into it and puts on the flashers.

We leave the TV in the Subaru and scope out the situation. Even from the handicapped spot, the sister's front door is fifty yards away. We cross a minefield of slush, frozen into ruts hidden under a fresh drape of eight inches of snow.

"We can't carry it that far." I say that much out loud. *We'll slip, the television will land on top of us, and from our new perspective of traction in twin hospital beds, we'll wish all you had were two bad knees.*

Bob moves toward the front door, lifting each footstep up and out of snow. He rings the doorbell. We wait. And wait. *If she's not here I will . . . I will what?* Fury mounts in my head.

The door swings open. Before us stands a woman, seventy-five maybe. Thin, straggly gray hair falls into her face as she leans from her walker to grasp the door handle. Shapeless clothing covers the mounds of her body. Navy blue stretch pants stretch across haunches the size of motorcycle tires. Weak eyes peer from behind glasses. Behind her, I see a tiny living room, brightly lit, crammed with stuff, a narrow rabbit trail leading in.

My pique vanishes. We are looking at the face of poverty. I'm flooded with shame. All day, I have thought only of myself, of how Bob's instinctive helpfulness has inconvenienced me. My shame is like a light switch flipping my focus from me to the woman in front of us. Bob never thinks of himself. Helping others is built into him. Apparently, I need to meet a stranger face-to-face to make the human connection.

The woman introduces herself: Charlene.

"Didn't think you'd come tonight after all, with this storm," Charlene says, turning and shuffling her walker down the rabbit trail. She can barely make her way through the clutter, piled floor nearly to ceiling. We follow. Furniture, magazines, boxes form canyon walls within the room. If we stand on tiptoe, we see over the piles that she already owns a defunct big-screen TV against one wall.

It dawns on me that we have to move that first.

"Okay," I say brightly. "Perhaps Bob and I can move this, ah . . ." Where? I see sliding-glass patio doors beyond the heap. "Outdoors! On your covered patio!" I worm my way over and look out. The tiny, cement-block patio is crammed with an ancient, rusting grill on wheels, tumbled webbed aluminum lawn furniture, and box upon box, snow blasting everything.

"We'll make room out there, then move your old big-screen outside, *then* move the new one in," I say.

Charlene grips her walker as we shift and clear, eventually unearthing yet another, smaller television. Charlene shuffles behind her walker. "Could you put that smaller TV in the bedroom?"

"I'll do that." *Think strong.* I wrap my arms around the set, lifting with my legs, as Charlene motions toward the bedroom. It's down the hall from where we came in, blocked by a birdcage I hadn't seen earlier. With two live birds in it. Bob lifts the cage out of the way and I back into the bedroom, hugging the TV, waddling under its weight.

The bedroom is filled by a queen-size bed, heaped with clothes, mashed up against two walls. Charlene motions to the bed's far side. I can see a crate atop a cabinet. "Put that TV over there," she instructs.

There's no room to walk around the bed. I remind myself this woman needs help. We've been sent through a snowstorm for this purpose. I hug the TV tighter, lay down on the bed, roll over and over again, and plop the TV on the crate.

"Could you connect it too?" Charlene asks.

"Sure, I can do that." Bob joins me, rolling over the bed to get to the little telly. Lying flat, reaching down into the well under the TV, crate, and cabinet, he somehow makes it work.

It takes another twenty minutes to move Charlene's old big-screen from the living room out onto the patio, but finally space is cleared and we can start the job we came for.

Our Subaru is a long way from Charlene's front door, a vast parking lot away, a prairie away, a prairie experiencing a blizzard of pioneer-day proportions. But now, as the two of us maneuver our giant screen out of the hatchback, stepping in unison through deep snow, I feel our purpose. My husband, who lives the golden rule as naturally as he breathes, is my example.

Charlene is waiting by the front door and swings it wide—well, as wide as she can with a birdcage behind it—to let us in. Step, step, turn, and the two of us lower the screen into place in the living room. I stand, rubbing the small of my back, as Bob sets it up. I cannot imagine making sense of the wires and plugs, but he does. I search for the remote, and hold it aloft triumphantly as he snaps the last connection together. I can just make out a recliner under a pile in a corner. I clear dishes and clothes off so Charlene can sit.

"Here's how to work it." Bob leans down to Charlene, starting a tutorial, as the TV pops to life, the talking heads of a Seattle newsroom suddenly loud and lively in this tiny box of a living room. I'm ready to go, but Charlene isn't ready to release us.

"What if I have trouble with it in the future?"

"Why don't I write my cell right here on the instruction manual?" Bob scribbles his name and number in his engineer's block script. "Call me if you need help."

We turn and weave through Charlene's maze of a living room, retracing the rabbit trail. We're done, we're happy, we're happy that we're done. At the door, we shift the birdcage out of the way so we can open it. We turn and see Charlene in the recliner, her walker to one side, watching the newscasters in Seattle going on about the weather. Quite a snowstorm, they say. Quite a connection, Bob and I affirm with a nod, as we close the door behind us.

Cheryl Stritzel McCarthy is a journalist in Bellingham, Washington, who freelances for The Wall Street Journal, Chicago Tribune, *and* Los Angeles Times. *Her book* Many Hands Make Light Work, *is a rollicking memoir — currently open for agency — about growing up in a boisterous Catholic family in the Midwest in the sixties and seventies.*

Not Native

Carol McMillan

Although I have slept, eaten, laughed, argued, peed, made love, and prayed on the Colville Tribe's Reservation off-and-on for more than thirty years, I am not Native. To my knowledge, I'm approximately seventy-five percent Highland Scot. We're tribal people. Our clans subsisted on salmon and deer for thousands of years. Maybe that's a tiny piece of why the Colville Reservation feels like home to me. Eastern Washington tribes are deer and salmon people too.

When I came back from my first trip to Scotland, where I learned the history of the Clearances and other atrocities committed against the Highlanders by the conquering English, I ranted on and on to the small group of Nez Perce speakers in the Tribe's language program that I'd been working with for several years.

"It was the same thing! The British forbade us to wear our tartans, to play the bagpipes, to speak our language, to practice our religion. Highlanders are tribal. Our land was stolen. I am here because my ancestors were kicked off our native land. I visited places where they have standing stones that people I'm descended from must have carried many miles in order to erect into sacred circles. We subsisted on salmon and deer. It's the same story as here!"

The group was silent after my tirade. Then Albert Andrews, who often portrays himself as a "traditional" stoic Indian, said in his most traditionally stoic voice, "What's the matter with you? Didn't you ever see *Braveheart*?"

We all laughed. I love Indian humor.

* * *

There are times I forget that I'm non-Indian. My friend, Sheila Timentwa, wanted to adopt me as her sister. She took me to her Northern Cheyenne reservation at Lame Deer, Montana, to ask her mother for a deceased relative's Indian name that she could give to me, as was the custom in her tribe. We traveled in early December. A small group of antelope disappeared through scattered pines as we rolled into the driveway of Sheila's sister Louella's frame home. The long ride and sunny day prompted Sheila to suggest a walk into town after we greeted her relatives. Sheila led me on a tour of the small town's center. The peeling paint of the buildings reflected the difficult lives of its residents. Few sources of income existed on the rez. By the time we returned to her sister's house, the darkened air chilled us deeply. We rolled in blankets and slept on the floor with many of Sheila's female relatives. That night the temperature dropped to forty below zero. The neighbor's horse froze to death in his corral.

For the next few days, we huddled around a card table set up before the open fireplace. Louella was renowned for her exquisite beading. She and Sheila helped me with my pitiful, lumpy beading while we watched *National Lampoon's Christmas Vacation* over and over, until we could laugh at and quote all the best lines in the movie.

One of the children ran around the living room squeezing a strange little plastic figure that had a hideously ugly face. During one pass, he put it down on our table. Louella picked it up, scrutinizing its twisted face.

"This is what my boyfriend looks like when he comes."

Hilarity. Louella's observation became the phrase of our week. When one of the men came out of their back room to throw another log onto our fire, we'd all explode into laughter again.

The sky outside stayed crystal blue, but whenever a person opened the front door to stamp in from the frigid day, water vapor condensed out of the moist living room air, creating an instantaneous indoor snowstorm. In order to keep my car running, Sheila's relatives put it into their garage with a lightbulb burning beside the ignition switch. I became the taxi for any necessary errands. Sheila's mother, Elva Stands-in-Timber, chose to stay with us during the extreme weather. I drove Elva thirty miles out to her home so she could be certain her water was turned off. During the journey, she recounted stories of winters on the rez when she was a child. Everything had its season then, and cultural stories were passed on in the winter. Her dad gave each of his children traditional stories to learn. He'd tell a story four nights in a row, then the recipient would tell it for the next four, getting errors corrected each night. By the eighth night, the story would have been successfully passed to the next generation.

Elva told me, as we were passing a big field, that it had been the grounds for the Christmas pow-wows. The family would ride in a sleigh with their tee-pee and food for a week loaded onto a pile of hay in the back. The kids would burrow into the hay, sneaking out when their parents weren't watching in order to ride on the back runners as they slid through the snow. Elva said she never remembered being cold. When they reached the pow-wow grounds, the children's job was to shovel out a circle for the tee-pee, then fill it with hay, so that once the tee-pee was set up, their feet and bedding never touched the frozen ground.

Elva looked over at me, then back outside the car window. "My grandmother told me a story of her childhood. She had a memory from when she was very little of her mother dragging her through a creek. They were running. She wondered why her mother was trying to drown her. She heard what she later realized were shots being fired."

Elva looked down. I wondered if any of my ancestors, who had lived in the Midwest at that time, might have been firing those shots. I wondered at the poignant miracle of us being together in my car at that moment. All whites who spend time on a rez must struggle past inevitable white guilt.

While we'd all been beading at Sheila's sister's house, Elva also had been teaching me how to sew Cheyenne moccasins. When we reached her home, she went to the basement to check on the water. Elva returned with an old cardboard suitcase. Opening it, she shook out a large, gray piece of buckskin with long, thin strips. "This was my grandmother's wedding dress." Picking up a pair of scissors, Elva snipped two slender pieces off the end. As she rubbed them with fine sandpaper, the strips changed from gray to snowy white. "You need laces for those moccasins. These will do." Since that time, I have worn holes in the soles of those moccasins from dancing intertribal dances at countless pow-wows. I have knotted and mended those frayed laces many times, but I will never replace them.

On the final day of our stay in Lame Deer, I went to the grocery for a few items. Handing the clerk money, I was so shocked looking at my hand that I nearly jerked it back into my sleeve. The hand I saw was a puny pale color with some darker spots, nothing like the beautiful chestnut skin I'd been surrounded by for a week. It was the first time I'd forgotten that I was non-Indian.

The Indian name that we had traveled to find never got discussed, at least not within my hearing. Sheila told me that finding the right name for me was a process, and her mother would think seriously about it. In the Cheyenne tradition, only one person carries a name at a time. The name that was given to me a year later, in an elaborate ceremony at the Nez Perce longhouse on the Colville Reservation, was last carried by Sheila's father's great-aunt, *nistoyxa*. Receiving the name *nistoyxa* conferred upon me all the power put into it by the previous women who had carried it. A gift beyond measure.

* * *

There are undoubtedly many people who think I'm a wannabe, a white person who wishes she were Indian. Maybe, but I think I know too well what it means to be Indian to actually want that. Being Indian requires a larger dose of courage than I have ever owned. Indians learn to acknowledge internalized shame and colonization while constantly battling to rid their lives of its gnawing, insidious destruction. Indian men catch fish and hunt to feed people, especially at ceremonies. Indian women dig roots, gather and preserve berries to feed people, especially at ceremonies. Indian children look out for their elders, seeing that they have firewood for the winter, salmon in their freezers, plates of food at gatherings. All the while attempting to resist, or being unable to resist, the ubiquitous temptations of drugs and alcohol. But of course, some Indians do none of those things.

Sheila's husband, Bill, is a leader in the Walashut longhouse, the traditional religion of Chief Joseph's band of the Nez Perce. Bill once told me that it's a lot of work to be Indian. Following traditions, the drummers sometimes visit the dying to sing special songs, helping them through the process. After a tribal member has died, the singers stay up all night at the three-day funeral. Their songs take care of the deceased until the soul is sent off. After the body is interred at dawn on the third day, the mourners return to the longhouse to participate in a crying ceremony. Here the tears are finally released, when they can no longer be dropped onto the skin of the deceased where they would have burned painfully. The survivors' tears will no longer keep their loved one back from the journey they must embark upon. The drummers and singers actively support every aspect of the funeral.

No, mostly, Indian life is too difficult for me to be a true wannabe. The fact of my white skin confers privileges that I would not want to nor be able to give up even if I tried. Being non-Native, I will never know the vastness of that privilege. As a fish will never understand water, I simply live in white privilege. Policemen don't assume I'm a criminal; waitresses don't ignore me in restaurants; people don't want to steal my babies or touch my hair. Even on the rez, when confronted by someone's hatred of whites, I have a bubble of protection that people of color do not. We all know there are stronger penalties for harming a white person than for others in this country. I battle to understand the infinite aspects of white privilege that affect every piece of daily life, while wishing for a world in which there were no such distinctions.

But here's a racist statement: I love Indians. Maybe I should just say I love aspects of Indian culture. Not just the longhouse ceremonies that are every bit as soul-filling as white people think they must be, but even more, the self-deprecating humor of the rez. On the rez I am laughed at and I can laugh at myself. I understand the privilege of being allowed to share in that culture.

* * *

After hearing about Sheila for many years, when my biological sister, Jean, came to visit me, she wanted to meet her. We drove thirty miles to the reservation town of Nespelem, down Sheila's dirt driveway, climbed a few steps onto her plywood porch, and were welcomed into her typical rez home. Blankets gifted at ceremonies formed a neat stack in a corner, framed photos of the family graced the living room walls, and beadwork-in-progress sat on a folding TV table. We all settled onto the lumpy couch covered with a Pendleton blanket. After a few moments of polite conversation, Sheila looked pointedly at my sister.

"You know, don't you, that we were never noble and we were never savages." Sheila laughed, succinctly explaining away Indian stereotypes for my sister. Jean joined in Sheila's laughter.

I've never forgotten the depth of truth in her statement. I identify. I am not Native, but I, too, am not noble, nor am I savage. I like this as a baseline for humanity.

Carol McMillan has been published in academic journals but moving to Bellingham brought out her love for poetry and prose. She is the author of one book, White Water, Red Walls, *and has been published in several anthologies. She is currently working on a memoir of 1960s Berkeley.*

Nineteenth Province

Kenneth Meyer

23 February 1991

The petrol-moat was a hundred meters in front of Captain Taleb's trench, and beyond that lay the minefield. Finally, a half-kilometer to the west was the enemy berm, a four-meter-high sand-barrier extending thirty kilometers north and south. Who knew what was going on behind it, but Taleb supposed it wasn't anything good. So much depended upon, well, time. He didn't know how much time they had as he regarded the petrol-moat, the minefield, and the enemy-built berm, but he thought they didn't have much.

His 300-man company was already reduced to 225 men, with fifty having deserted (but good luck with that, since the disciplinary *fawj*, or battalion, was patrolling to the rear) and another twenty-five having been wounded in the bombardments. If the bombardment continued for another day or two, how many would remain? The enemy coalition might arrive to find few were present to defend Iraq's nineteenth province. Since no one could hear your thoughts, Taleb reflected ruefully that that project had gone less than smashingly. There was universal agreement that the Kuwaiti former ruling family had been no collection of heroes, but the local population had shown absolutely no enthusiasm for the nineteenth province business. On the contrary, now there was the mostly ineffective but nevertheless bothersome Kuwaiti resistance.

There was a second defensive line ten kilometers back, manned by a skeleton force, but if there was a massive attack, would they have time to get to it? And would it make any difference?

At twenty hundred hours he called Group Central in Kuwait City, but when he asked for the brigadier, he was told that officer wasn't available. "Give me Natiq," demanded Taleb, a captain he knew.

"This is Natiq."

"*Wawie.*" Jackal. Use of the assigned call signs among the officers was inconsistent, but Taleb liked his. "Where is the brigadier?"

"Ah, *wawie.*" Low: "*Rah ya rajil.*" He went, man.

Not "he went to another post," or "he's in a conference," but "he went."

"*Batigh.*" Watermelons! In other words, you're kidding me . . .

"*Mu batigh ya rajil, w'allahi.*" No kidding, man, I swear to God. Taleb understood that Natiq wasn't volunteering any lengthy narrative because you never knew when the *Istakhbarat*, or military intelligence, might be listening.

"Are there any updates?"

"There has been no ground attack. All units hold position."

"I'll check in again at oh eight hundred hours. *Fi amanallah.*" God keep you safe.

"*Fi amanallah.*"

Taleb didn't say he would check in the next day, because there was no day or night now: twenty hours ago, his comrades had fired the al-Burqman wells ten kilometers to the rear. The reasoning of the Supreme Commander in Baghdad was apparently: "If we can't have the oil, no one can!" Now there was only a sooty twilight.

The petrol-moat ignited just before dawn on the morning of 24 February. A five-meter-high wall of flames now loomed in front of the company.

"Prepare to receive the enemy," Taleb passed down the line.

There were explosions fifteen kilometers to the north, but no attack came in their sector. Taleb had called Group Center as soon as he saw the petrol-moat light up, but there was no answer. The command post in Kuwait City was being jammed or had been taken out in an air strike. He then called Sami to the north, who commanded the next company in the line. He had known Sami in the last war, the Iran-Iraq war.

"This is *wawie.*"

"Sami here." He heard explosions in the background; it sounded like the line was cutting out, but Taleb knew the difference.

"*Shaku maku Sami.*" How are you Sami? "When did we light up the moat?"

Sami chuckled. "*Eini.*" My eye, a common Iraqi endearment. "It was the Americans who touched off the moat. In Jamal's sector." The company to the north of Sami. "Then they came over the berm in armored bulldozers, plowed sand into the canal and into Jamal's trenches too. Five minutes later a column of three hundred tanks flew by. They didn't bother to engage us but proceeded east. We have over a hundred of Jamal's boys in our trenches now. The remnants."

"That's good."

The Iraqi command had thought that the struggle for Kuwait would develop along the lines of the 1980-1988 Iran-Iraq war—a drawn-out engagement with fortified lines, layers of defenses, and so on. Hence the hunkering down in the trenches. Now it seemed ridiculous.

"What are you going to do?"

"We're reading our leaflets." The enemy had dropped thousands of Arabic language leaflets starting out with the inviting phrase, *If you want to live* . . . The left-hand side of the paper depicted a soldier with a Saddam-style mustache thinking of his family, pictured above his head. Then on the right-hand side of the paper came the instructions: *Come forward with your weapons slung over your left shoulder, barrel-down, hands raised above your head. As you near our positions, make no sudden moves.* Taleb had read the leaflet, and so had the rest of the company.

"I can't raise Group Central," admitted Taleb.

"*Naqdoohum!*" Screw them! "My friend, I think the war just ended. Adil at Group Central told me last night the brigadier had gone. He didn't move, he didn't withdraw, he just went. But we will hold this position for the moment. Do as you think best."

"*Shoofak badain insha'allah, ya Sami.*" See you later, God-willing, Sami.

"*Fi Amanallah!*" Taleb replaced the receiver and considered the road north from Al Jahrah to the Iraqi border. It was the only four-lane highway leading into Iraq and the fastest way to go, but it was logical that if some units tried to make use of the highway, the Americans would turn it into the world's largest shooting gallery. Taleb shuddered.

He called Lieutenant Shukri to him. "We're mounting up. Get all the men into the APCs, including the wounded." The company had fifteen roadworthy Russian-made BTR-80s. They were only rated to carry thirteen men each, but what was left of the company could squeeze into the vehicles they had. "The enemy is already driving into Kuwait City. We'll pull back to the second line." If the second line was still there. Perhaps no one was manning that line now, but it was certain the company was fulfilling no useful function sitting by the blazing canal.

They had been on the road for all of five minutes and it was one of the rare times Taleb was not in the lead vehicle. He was wondering how that had happened when the APC in front of him exploded. His driver went around the wreckage and increased speed.

"Airborne platform, sir," reported the radioman behind him. That meant helicopters or a slow-moving plane, and both were bad.

"Pull over the column and get all the men out. Form a perimeter." For what that was worth.

The radioman, whose name was Qasim, looked at him in surprise. Qasim had no doubt forgotten the lecture from ten months ago. Of course no one wanted to leave the armored vehicles, that was a given, but in this situation you had to.

"If we don't get out, they'll destroy the fifteen vehicles with us sitting in them!" explained Taleb tersely. "Move!" The APCs were designed to protect the men from small-arms fire or the occasional rocket-propelled grenade, not heavy ordnance dropped from above. The radioman relayed the orders. "*Al eini wa ra'si,*" By my eye and head! came back the replies, in other words: right away!

Taleb had barely stepped out of the APC and was bending over to run into a depression when something plucked his sleeve and spun him around. It felt like someone had jabbed a spear point into his left shoulder. He still made it into the ditch. He realized he was bleeding and managed not to faint, taking deep breaths.

"Thirteen of the fifteen APCs were successfully evacuated," reported the radioman. Qasim was sticking close by him, as he was supposed to.

So, 195 men were on the ground. No one, including Taleb, wanted to die for Iraq's nineteenth province, or for that matter, for Saddam.

"Enemy ground troops engaging."

That was obvious. "Return fire." He just hoped it wasn't the Emiratis or the Syrians. It would be too galling to surrender to them. The Syrians had supported the Iranians during the last war and in the UAE he supposed an armored vehicle was probably something they used to go to the shopping mall.

He wondered where the Egyptians were. It was known that Mubarak had sent two divisions to fight on the enemy side. This was odd because it was not much of a secret that during the Iran-Iraq war, some Egyptian units had been in Iraq to lend a hand. That conflict had ended in August 1988, but it was possible there were some Egyptians driving towards Kuwait City now who had been fighting side by side with Iraqis not long ago.

All these useless thoughts vanished in an instant: his objective now was simply to save as many men as possible.

The company medic, Bashir, crawled over and after examining and bandaging Taleb pronounced, "Captain, I sentence you to live." That was a typical utterance for Bashir. "Keep pressure on it. That one went right through. It smarts though, eh?"

"You know it does."

"I'll be back," was all the medic said before disappearing.

Taleb suddenly realized the enemy was no longer firing. "Cease fire, cease fire," he directed to the radioman. "Wait." The small-arms fire died down, then ended.

Someone was calling through a bullhorn in standard Arabic. "This is Captain McKay of the Second Armored Division, U.S. Army. Come forward with your weapons slung over your left shoulder and your arms raised. You have one minute." And then the message repeated.

There was no accent, so Taleb thought that had to be an interpreter, he supposed a Saudi. The three soldiers around him regarded him expectantly. They were good boys.

This was it then. "Faris, you have the best English." Taleb had only studied some Russian. He passed the private a white handkerchief. "Sling your weapon over your left shoulder, wave the white cloth, and tell them we're coming out. Tell them we have wounded." *Including me.* "Radio: tell everyone to wait till they hear Faris make contact, then walk out slowly. Follow the instructions from the leaflet." After those orders had been relayed:"In fact, give me the microphone." The radioman handed it over. "This is the captain. Let's get out of this ditch. Move slowly. Out."

Now they could hear Faris calling to the enemy.

Taleb handed back the microphone. "That's it. Let's go boys. You there." He lifted his chin at a corporal. "I can't raise my left arm. Let me lean on you when we stand up."

The corporal regarded him in alarm, and Taleb knew just what he was thinking: are we all going to be shot by the enemy?

"*La thaef jundi, yala!*" Don't worry soldier. Let's go.

"Don't drag it out," he added.

Although currently an enthusiastic resident of Washington State, Kenneth Meyer spent most of his adult life overseas. He has a continuing interest in China, Greece, and the Middle East—in particular, the Arab world. He resided for several years in Egypt, Iraq, and Tunisia.

Reframing

Linda Morrow

Head down, sunglasses pushed up over my forehead, I move my sandaled feet slowly along the beach just below the wrack line on a late September afternoon. Tiny insects, sand fleas perhaps, swarm around wet, dusky-green seaweed. Golden beams dance on gentle wavelets under cobalt blue sky. I am seeking solace and solitude and the deserted shoreline does not disappoint. Today, September 27, 2017, marks the fifty-first birthdate of my first-born son and the second year I've grieved his passing. I've dreaded the approach of this day. Yesterday was the worst. A lump sat heavy in my gut all day and tears flowed without warning. Today seems easier. I hadn't planned to come here, but trust the ocean and her shores to give me what I need—she always has. The receding waters of the outgoing tide paint the small stones and pebbles glistening shades of butterscotch-gold, creamy-white, blue-grey, jet-black.

My eyes consider the pink rubber bracelet on my left wrist—Steve's favorite color—where white letters spell *What am I—chopped liver?* the words he always knew just when to use to get a laugh. In the spring of 2016, I ordered five hundred of these bracelets to promote a fundraising effort to honor Steve when I ran a leg of the Burlington Vermont City Marathon—the place he'd lived for the last twenty years of his life.

A few nights ago, as I removed a faded band before getting into bed, it snapped and broke. I'd replaced this talisman several times since the race, when I gave it away—spontaneously, but with intention—sometimes to a friend, sometimes to a stranger, because I felt a connection between Steve and the individual. But that evening, as I held the broken rubber strand in my hand, I wondered, "Are you telling me something, Steve? Are you okay? Is it time to let go?" I ended up taping the worn bracelet in my journal. The next morning, I put on a fresh one—the last from the original order.

As I continue along the shoreline, I begin picking up stones—small egg-shaped ones, polished smooth by years of tumbling waves, shimmering wet from the salty brine. One by one, these treasures find their way into the pockets of my khaki shorts. I seem to know exactly which ones to pluck among infinite choices. Bend and gather, bend and gather, bend and gather. The shoreline curves, and I can no longer see the huge driftwood logs marking the spot where I began. Along a narrowing beach, a single scarlet leaf separates from an overhanging branch and pirouettes down and down before landing on the coarse sand. A lone seagull wheels and squawks then settles gracefully a few yards off shore, bobbing with the eternal rhythm of the waves. I continue my walking, my quest, trusting I will know when to stop, when to turn back.

And then I am done. I turn and begin to retrace my steps. I lower my glasses to shield my eyes from the low-hanging sun. In the distance rise the rugged peaks of the Canadian Coastal Mountains, their snow-tipped fingers reaching towards the heavens. I feel a subtle shift within me. A kind of energy rises from my feet and flows upward through my torso. My body relaxes. The lump in my throat loosens. I am light and floating. Breathe in, breathe out. Walking, walking.

I am surprised when I find myself straddling the girth of a silver-gray log, and spot the break in the brush indicating the path to the paved parking lot where I left my car. I look at my watch, 5:00 pm. I've been walking along the shoreline for three hours. One hand goes to my throat and reaches for the sterling pendent I put on every morning. Fingertips run over the ridges on the front side of the oval. I close my eyes feeling the lines of each seashell, the curve of the waves, the single starfish. My thumb rubs the smooth backside where Steve's ashes are suspended in clear resin. "You are always with me, Steve. Happy Birthday, Buddy."

Mechanically, I begin extracting the stones I've collected from my bulging pockets. Carefully I place each one on the smooth weathered surface of this fallen giant. Now dry, the pieces have lost their rich luster, but they are remarkably similar in shape and size. I stare down at my collection, marveling at the oval shapes so like the pendant my hand enclosed. After a few moments of silent contemplation, I place each stone in a nylon bag, pull the drawstring and leave the beach, heading for my car. Thoughts of my son continue to wash over me.

I didn't expect to have Steve long—certainly not for forty-nine years. When he was born with Down syndrome and a congenital heart defect, his pediatrician told me, "Your baby is a little Mongoloid." Then he added that Steve was "unlikely to outlive his teens." But that doctor didn't know the depth of Steve's soul. Nor could he measure the tenacity that allowed Steve to rise above the crests of life's waves, even the biggest ones. Not only did he compensate for his lifelong heart issues, but Steve also navigated the storm of an aneurysm on his brain at age thirty-eight. Several years later, a stroke caused temporary paralysis in Steve's right arm and permanent damage to his dominant right hand. Slowly, sometimes amid salty tears of frustration, my son persisted and relearned to write and draw with his left hand. Steve had as much grit in him as the grains of sand on the beach I just walked.

On the half-hour drive home, a new possibility begins to take shape. Murky edges gain definition. *What if, what if . . . what if I saw September 27 — Steve's birthdate — in a different way? What if . . . instead of grieving for my son, I saw this date as a day to celebrate him and all he stood for? A life lived without judgment, and copious amounts of unconditional love. A personality imbued with an impeccable sense of humor, genuine kindness, and unlimited gratitude. An individual brimming with determination, resiliency, courage, and yes, just a bit of stubbornness.* For me, someone who typically sees the glass as half empty, this is a huge paradigm shift. So much depends on perspective!

Steve saw the world in which he lived without filters. Often he revealed the wisdom he carried within him through his unique way of expressing himself, referred to by our family as "Steve-isms." Who hasn't felt "happy-sad" when conflicting emotions roil and tumble in our gut? And what about feeling "a teeny bit nervous" when confronting a new or challenging situation? A steep path ahead — either literally or figuratively — becomes "a heavy hill." And don't we all wish we could "do it again, more often" after a great meal with friends or a perfect vacation?

Back home, I head straight to the cabinet where I keep the tributes people shared with me about Steve. As I reread the comments contained in condolence cards, certain words and phrases appear with steadfast consistency. People remember Steve as "a teacher," "a light," "a jokester," "joyful," "kind-hearted." Next, I turn the pages of the guest register we used for Steve's Celebration of Life—a book titled *On Morning Wings.* Vermont author Reeve Lindbergh created the text, a gentle adaptation of Psalm 139. The illustrations follow four children through a playful day, and when one of them feels lost or lonely, the other friends are always close by.

Among the many signatures and expressions of love, my eyes linger on one in particular. *Steve, you left a legacy of spunk, humor, determination, and love. For this we are thankful. You were a blessing in our lives.* The statement captures the essence of Steve. Finally, I reach for a gift given to me at the celebration by a woman, a close friend of one of Steve's brothers. My fingers close around an action figure of Captain America. Around his neck hangs a paper shield she created with the words: *Super Hero Steve—With the powers of love, generosity, joy, and goodness.*

I close my eyes and center my breathing. Can I use these attributes to reframe how I mark Steve's birthdate in the years to come? In a world where we increasingly define individuals by differences rather than similarities, can I use my son's memory to find the good? I think of the people in my life who knew Steve and loved him. They are many: the woman in Arizona who knew Steve his entire life and referred to him as her *Anam Cara*, an old Gaelic term meaning "soul friend"; the award-winning chef in New York City who remembered Steve as "my link to foods like baloney sandwiches on white bread and a can of Tab, items that were verboten in my whole foods house"; the artist in Los Angeles who works for Pixar Animation Studios and befriended him when they were in the same classroom in elementary school; the teenage boy in St. Johnsbury, Vermont, who was a ten-year-old when he first met my son, and subsequently declared, "Steve is one of my best friends," who wore his chopped-liver bracelet for over a year until it disintegrated; the eighty-year-old in Syracuse, New York, who fed Steve his first taste of ice cream when he was an infant and now struggles each day to live with the confusion of Alzheimer's. I especially remember the author in Burlington, Vermont, Steve's steadfast friend who roamed the city with him. Together they went bowling, shopping at Goodwill and shared a similar taste in movies. He also introduced Steve to the "chopped liver" phrase. So many individuals, leading such disparate lives, spread across our country, but in my mind united by their connection to Steve, a connection that taught them to enjoy life's simplest things.

I wonder. On Steve's birthdate, could I reach out to one person each year, send the individual a sum of money equivalent to Steve's would-be age, and ask that the money be used to perform one small act in honor of Steve and what he meant to him or her? In that way, Steve's birthday will truly be celebrated with joy in my heart and in others.

Eventually I cease my meditation and open my eyes. I gaze out the windows of my home where the sun has dipped below the horizon, and the waters of Bellingham Bay reflect a blushing cloud-filled sky tinged with hues of vibrant orange, rose, and dusky purple. The sharp images in my mind soften, curl into a wisp of thought, and drift away. But the concept remains. I know that Steve has given me a gift and a slice of his wisdom. He would not want me to be morose or sad on this, his day. He would note my poor attitude and gently reprimand me with our family's favorite Steve-ism, "That's not very Disney."

I have a year to figure out how I will mark his birthday. What action will I take to honor Steve's goodness and grace? Surely, I will save some of that day to return to the beach, to walk and give silent thanks. I will always miss my son. I will always grieve his passing. And on the date of his birth, I will always be glad he lived.

A native of New England, Linda Morrow moved to the Pacific Northwest in 2013 to be closer to family and find community. Bellingham easily met those expectations, although she continues to cheer (loudly) for the Red Sox and the Patriots. More about Linda and her work can be found at her website LMorrow.com

Cri de Coeur

Marla Morrow

The overhead triplet of electric lightbulbs glares a harsh awakening. My mother's small hands clench her crossed arms that press against her large breasts, not yet cupped by a white cotton bra. She's rolling from side to side on the frigid linoleum floor. Her knee-length housecoat of pastel pink and soft blue flowers has become a field of terror. She's trapped in the kitchenette by my lunatic father within three sides of varnished wooden cupboards and drawers that store cheap metal pots and pans, faded towels, a roll of waxed paper, tangled rubber bands, and a ball of salvaged string.

There is no escape from this angular snare.

My father towers over her, kicking my mother with his heavy boots. They're scuffed brown leather and are laced in taut even X's. The side of his face is crimson. Purple and blue veins pulse madly upon it. His laughter roars and my mother's breasts crack with each blow and make odd sounds of splintering tissue I've never heard before, again and again.

This is all I hear.

My father's glass eye stares without emotion as he foams at the mouth, enraged. Brownish-yellow bubbles cluster in the corners and slide down his chin onto my mother, my mommy. He drives his boots into her like blows of a splitting maul into a burled round of birch. He's a woodsman. He reeks of chainsaw gasoline.

My mother's face lies beneath a mask of sweat. She only moans. Now, I think she must not have wanted to frighten me more than I was nor give my father the pleasure of her screams to stop, of pain and fear, of breaking down. But then, the screams begin, loud and louder, a crescendo of amplified agony. "Stop! Stop! For God's sake, stop!"

I am seven, living in a body of skinny, mostly bones, with tousled blonde hair and blue eyes. I am the baby of three. I, the youngest, his favored child, must find a weapon to assault my father, my daddy, this frothing, wildly insane monster. I think of the canister vacuum cleaner and its metal tubes that are kept behind the door not far from me, not far from where my father drools, not far from where my mother sobs and rolls back and forth, now curling into a battered ball, a shattered woman. My mother, a goddess of slivered glass. I want to strike my father. Across his back! Across his face as he turns fully toward me in surprise! Even across his skull to fall him! But I am as hollow and useless as a vacuum cleaner tube would be. I do not move. I hate myself, my weakness, my immobility, my pale skin that only stretches across bones, not strong musculature, and I hate my pink flannel nightgown that floats around me, but most of all, I hate my father.

I hear his red pickup truck start and rumble to the stop sign at 23rd Avenue. Then, he shifts gears into away.

My mother crouches on the floor. I rush toward her. "Mommy! Mommy!" I whimper. She slowly stands. I cling to her as she staggers down the hall toward the master bedroom and crawls underneath the blankets. I lean into her. "Mommy?" I ask. There is no reply. I rest my face near hers. She is still. Her shallow breath is warm upon my forehead. It comforts me.

That afternoon, Mother hobbles to the rotary phone in our kitchen. She dials numbers and makes appointments for herself on the following day with our family physician and Reverend.

I'm hiding where I can easily watch them undetected. The Reverend's ledged on the button-backed couch in our living room. His black wool trilby is set beside him. The Reverend wipes the top of his head as if his hair is out of place, but he's bald and the only thing that's out of place is him in our home. His posture is rigid and squared. He's dressed in a black suit and his white shirt collar is a luminescent ring that pinches his fat neck. His black tie is anchored by a silver cross tie tack. I look for Jesus nailed to it, but Jesus isn't there. The Reverend cradles a big black book with the words Holy Bible etched in gold on its spine.

The floor-length curtains are drawn to keep heat inside our house, but the wall thermometer only reads fifty-five degrees Fahrenheit. Frost patterns our single pane windows. We're out of heating oil. There's no money to bring the Frazier Oil delivery man here to fill our downstairs blue metal furnace that sits idle and cold. A table lamp with low wattage is on especially for the Reverend. In the daytime, we turn off all lights to save money on our electricity bill. Mother says every penny saved is a promissory copper salvation. I don't know what she means.

She sits on the matching love seat kitty-corner to the Reverend. Her soft brunette curls seem tired. My mother stretches her unfastened cardigan across her thinning body, pearlescent buttons to the left side, buttonholes on the right. A wadded white tissue is tucked underneath her turned-up sleeve cuff. Her shoulders droop. The Reverend locks his bespectacled eyes onto my mother's puffy blue eyes, half-circled with shades of gray beneath her lower eyelids.

"You did take the wedding vows, didn't you, June?"

"Yes, I did, but I didn't know that 'until death do you part' meant that I vowed to stay wed until he murdered me." My mother's breaths are shallow. She cautiously touches her taped ribs. "Now that I've replaced the door locks so that he can't come in, he's threatened to shoot me from outside while I'm sleeping. I've changed the headboard to a different wall, but . . . what then, Reverend? Who will care for the children? Their crazy father? Foster parents? Will they be torn apart, brother from sisters? Sister from sister? They need each other and they need me!"

I drop to hug my knees and stifle my sobs.

Mother fishes the tissue from her cuff and tears it into bits. "My children have seen heinous abuse, they've heard him bellow death threats, they're ribbed from hunger, they shake with cold." My mother's voice cracks and she pulls a throw across her lap to stop shaking from chill and recall. "He gives me a pittance that's not enough to care for their basic needs. They've seen him beat me and hold a hunting knife to my throat. He slit deep enough to spring blood. They're terrorized and you're telling me not to divorce this mad man? That we should stay together as a family? I will keep us together as a family, but *not* with him!"

The Reverend shoves our cat away that's come to rub against his pant leg. Then he smiles. "I've only known Don to be a kind and gentle man, always pleasant in conversation and a fine Christian in his nature and deed. What did *you* do to provoke such extreme behavior?" The Reverend opens his bookmarked Bible. "Hear the Word of God! 'Therefore what God has joined together, let no one separate. Mark 10:19.' You were joined with Don in covenant. If you divorce him, you'll be a shamed woman in society and as a parishioner. Your participation in the Christmas Eve program with your kindergarten class will be canceled and you won't be allowed to teach Sunday school anymore. Listen to I Timothy 2:12. 'But I suffer not a woman to teach, nor to usurp authority over the man, but to be in silence.' "

Mother slowly rises and minces steps to the front door. "Reverend, your pastoral counsel is of male superiority and lowly subservient women. I will continue teaching all children God's love, not God's judgment. Here," she seethes, "this door is open for you."

The Reverend slowly approaches Mother. "Woman, you are blasphemous. What I've sermonized is all-saving knowledge from the word of God which is my religious conviction. Do not taunt me."

Mother stands resolute before him. Her voice is solid. "This is *my* all-saving knowledge from the word of God. Like Jesus, I say 'Let the children come to me.' And the Song of Solomon 2:11 'I am the rose of Sharon, the lily of the valley.' I am *that* woman! I will bloom! I will flourish! I will thrive! My petals will be silken, my fragrance of honey and rose attar! Now is the time of my greatest beauty!"

Mother divorces father. Mother divorces the church. There's no more torment. I'm happy to stay home on Sunday mornings. I crawl into bed with Mother. We hold hands. Under the blankets, she's always warm.

She lets the children come to her. Little sweaty Eddie knocks on our front door. He has a speech impediment and his perpetually green snotty nose bubbles clusters that inflate and pop, glistening in the sunlight as they surround and fall upon us. My stomach loops, but Mother greets him with a lilt. "Hi Eddie!" She extends a Kleenex box. "Blow your nose," she commands. Eddie obeys and plops his weighted tissue into the wastebasket Mother offers, then jabs his hand into his pants pocket.

"Wanna nee my nake?" He pulls out a coiled garter snake by its tail. The reptile immediately elongates and pees.

"It's frightened," Mother says. "Let the beautiful devil go!"

In the divorce settlement, Mother wins a small alimony, child support, our house, and our 1956 Ford. She learns how to drive, unlike most other women. Mother is beautiful and bright. Both count. She secures a secretarial position at the Clark County Courthouse. Our hunger is mitigated. Mother buys heating oil and our house is finally warmed.

The delivery man's name is Axel. He looks very official in his uniform. Mother directs me downstairs to show Axel where our furnace is located. I listen to Mother singing so lovely in the kitchen and I listen to the furnace filling with oh, so lovely oil. Axel reignites the fuel light. I watch the bright blue flame hesitate in a flickering dance, then burn steady in its perfect shape and place. Axel tips his cap good-bye. I stand beside that big blue machine as it thunders back to life and I sing to it the pretty song Mother's singing upstairs.

In early spring, Axel knocks on our front door, removes his cap and mumbles an apology to Mother. The hose that must go through the basement window to reach the furnace tore blossoms off the camellia bush. He offers Mother a floral mound of pink.

"That's alright," Mother assures him. "You're thoughtful for arranging them into a beautiful bouquet for me!" Axel blushes, puts on his cap and drives to the next delivery. I'd seen him yank off the blossoms on the back side of the bush where he thought nobody'd see they'd been peeled off the branches. Mother's a gardener. She's aware of Axel's "accidental" overture. She cuts back the splintered branches with her sharp red-handled pruners. Summer's heat replaces Axel.

Time replaces time. Children grow. Decades pass. I'm sitting beside my mother in a nursing home. She lies in bed beneath bleached white linens. Her head rests upon a feeble prop of pillow. A worn platinum wedding band ringed with gold circles the third finger of her left hand. She married another, forty joyous years ago.

After her first stroke, contrary to her doctor's prophecy, Mother relearned how to walk and became an ebullient tap dancer. This stroke has rendered her dominant side flaccid. Death lurks. I struggle for discourse that's meaningful. What does one say to the dying? Mother stares at the dropped ceiling, then arduously turns toward me to speak. "Saint Augustine said, 'Come, Lord. Stir us up and call us back, kindle and seize us, be our fire and our sweetness. Let us love, let us run.' I loved your father," she says.

Marla Morrow, a published author, is proud to be the daughter of June Murray. Her mother's resolve, love of nature, fine and performing arts, reading, writing, children, four-leggeds, Japanese culture, and more have shaped her. A former Ferndale Arts Commissioner, Marla founded Hanadori Trail and Ferndale Cherry Blossom Festival.

Can You See Me Now?

Cheryl Nelson

It all depended upon the source. Information about the polio epidemic was shouted from newspaper headlines: *Polio hits New York City. Hundreds die.* The scientific community reported on the progress of research. The CDC encouraged everyone to be vaccinated. If asked, I would tell you that polio is my life story.

I am a polio survivor. I had infantile paralysis in 1956. I was three years old. I had two of the Salk three-shot series when I splashed in the contaminated neighborhood lake. The vaccine probably saved my life but it didn't stop my legs from being paralyzed. Some people would say that I was lucky. As luck would have it, I was in the hospital for three months. I lay in dark isolation for three days, struggled to learn to walk again, and left the hospital on crutches and in full leg braces.

I went into the hospital as a playful toddler, wearing overalls and a T-shirt. I came out three months later dressed in a white blouse and a starched satin jumper. I wore braces and ugly brown high-topped shoes. In the vernacular of the nineties, I lost my inner child. I was now a serious and determined little girl.

I enjoyed a somewhat protected and idyllic childhood. My dad built a sandbox low to the ground in our backyard. Friends from the neighborhood would come to build Disneyland in the sand with me. The girl who lived in the house behind us would come over almost every day. We would play cards and board games. If a bully did tease or taunt me, my little brother was usually willing to put up his fists and threaten to punch the culprit.

Most of my childhood friends accepted me as one of the group. They seemed to appreciate my sense of humor and my gung-ho spirit. I played street hockey in the neighborhood and foursquare on the school playground. I could hit the baseball with the best of my peers. There was usually more than one student who was willing to run the bases for me.

Things began to shift as we entered middle school. Our bodies were changing. Some of the boys' voices lowered. Many of the girls were developing breasts. It seemed that our physical appearance became a focus of our lives more and more. Meanwhile, I was able to walk without braces now, but my right leg did not change. It was shorter than my left and very skinny. I walked with a limp. I soon learned that this impediment was not considered attractive in the dating scene.

It was as if my right leg was the diagonal line across a circle indicating: *Not worthwhile*. Boys would ask my friends out while I was standing with them. Adults would ask someone in my family a question, then turn away if I answered. Kids called me "Lead foot." Many didn't believe me if I told a teacher that my legs hurt. They said that I was faking it so I could go home. Each insult, each time I was ignored or dismissed, I would grow more withdrawn. Another piece of me would disappear.

By the time I was in high school, I felt invisible. I wandered the halls like a ghost. I lived in the shadows. I was numb. I stayed after school and dragged my hands along the concrete walls until my knuckles bled. I doubt that anyone saw me. If they did, they didn't say anything. I started to skip classes. I thought no one would notice. They didn't care. I knew that they didn't want to see who lived inside of my crippled body.

I was invisible except when I wasn't. One young man that I dated told me that I wasn't as ugly as some of the girls. I assume that he meant that as a compliment. I was five foot four with hair the color of wheat. I always kept my hair cut short; it was easier to care for, especially after swimming. I loved the water. I could float in it. The water buoyed my weakened leg. I felt so much more at ease than when I walked on land. It seemed that everyone noticed my limp when I rushed from class to class.

I went to a Catholic high school. We all wore uniforms. I think the purpose was so that no one person would stand out, for good or for bad. I stood out, given my appearance and intelligence, for good and for bad. I'm so glad that we wore knee socks with our uniforms. At least they covered some of my legs.

I forced myself to function each day, made the effort for at least part of me to live. I was a member of the drama club, speech and debate, the pep club, and the National Honor Society. I participated in class discussions. One incident in our sophomore history class stands out. The teacher couldn't decide whether to throw the exam away because so many students failed or to record the scores because another student and myself earned over 100 percent. We had even answered the extra credit correctly. Everyone noticed us that day. We were deemed "teacher's pets."

I tried to exist somewhere in that gap between the ghost walker, the disabled body, and the "teacher's pet" persona. I tried to stand tall when the boys asked other girls out in front of me. I was intelligent and had a good sense of humor. But these were not the most important qualities for dating. So I withdrew even further.

There were some activities which pulled me out of myself for short periods of time, like the Friday night dances. Usually about 100 out of the 500 students in our school attended. We were mostly from white, middle- and working-class families. The faces at the dances were not very diverse. We were short, tall, dark-haired, some blonds and redheads. Everyone was able-bodied, except me.

The dances were a good time for my friends and me to gather outside of school hours. We lived in different neighborhoods. Most of us commuted to school from a distance. We talked on the phone but didn't get to hang out with each other very often.

One night we were standing and talking on one side of the dance floor. My friend, Sue, went to get a cup of punch for herself and for me. While I waited for her, I noticed a boy approaching me. I recognized him from some of my classes. I knew his name. I suppose he knew mine. But we weren't really friends.

Then there he was, standing in front of me. *This is awkward,* I thought. *Is he going to ask me to dance? Naw, he won't ask me. He knows about my leg. No one ever asks me to dance.* He did, though. I barely heard him when he said, "Do you wanna dance?"

He was sort of cute. He had short black hair and brown eyes. He was about an inch taller than me. I tried to remember what we had laughed about in our classes. Maybe we could just stand and have a conversation. He couldn't really want to dance with me. He had laughed one day when someone whispered, "She thinks she's so smart, but she can't even walk," after I passed them.

"Do you wanna dance?" he asked loudly. He was getting impatient. He would probably rather be with the other guys or a cuter girl, one without a gimpy leg.

"Sure," I told him. "Why not?"

The song was kind of slow, so he placed his hands loosely on my shoulders and I reached around his waist. A few phrases ran quickly through my head: I think I can do this. If I don't step on his toes. Please don't let me fall. We rocked slowly back and forth in time to the music. I began to relax. This was kind of fun. Didn't he think it was kind of fun? Then it happened. I should have known. I always tried to protect myself, brace myself against the words. Sticks and stones and all of that. This time I had begun to let my guard down. Bad idea.

"The vice principal told me to ask you to dance," he told me.

Great. What do you do now? harped the voice inside my head. I could have told you—no one wants a girl with a disability. Sure, you're smart and friendly. But you're just a buddy or someone people feel sorry for. Why do you even try? The voice clamored on and on.

"Stop," I exclaimed.

"What?"

"Stop, just stop. I, uh, I have to use the restroom."

Well, that's a new one, mocked the voice in my head. I don't want him to see me cry. He can't. He just can't. And off I ran, or tried to run.

I sped into one of the stalls in the bathroom, slammed and locked the door. I started to cry. When I was done sobbing, I resolved then and there never to let anyone know how much his words had hurt.

Monday at school was not very different. It was as if nothing had happened. But it had. I could do my best, be my best, even put my "best foot forward." People would still see who and what they chose to see.

I started to drink. I snuck into my parents' liquor cupboard after they went to bed and poured myself a glass of whiskey. It burned going down. I poured another one and chugged it. Pretty soon, the guy's comment didn't matter so much. Now, I was in control. I had a secret of my own. I had a tool, a way to fight back. I didn't have to care anymore.

First, it was just two or three drinks before I went to sleep. Then it was several in front of the TV late at night. Eventually, I drank cough medicine with alcohol before and after school. I cut my wrists. Nobody noticed. This was what I wanted, a solid wall of protection.

Then one day during April of our senior year, our high-school English teacher approached me. "The students and faculty took a vote and we would like you to address your graduating class. Frank will be valedictorian. You were elected as the other speaker," she stated.

I was shocked. I pulled myself together and replied, "Oh, okay. I would do that."

"You're welcome. You did well in speech and debate, and we appreciate all of the ways in which you support your peers and your school," she said. She turned and walked away.

Well, I'll be damned. They noticed you. Never saw that coming, the harsh voice inside of me commented.

Yes, they did. They are giving me the last word! I practiced my speech over the next six weeks. After four years, I would get to introduce who I really was. A sprout of hope grew through a crack in my wall.

* * *

I admit that I had a couple of drinks to celebrate before speaking. The priest announced my name. I limped across the stage and stood at the podium. My gait didn't matter quite so much tonight. Finally, the students and faculty saw me as more than my disability.

I closed my speech with this paraphrase from the choreographer and dancer, Martha Graham: "There is in each one of us an energy, a unique life force that is to be expressed. If it is not, it will be lost and gone forever."

Maybe that statement included me. I chose to believe that it did—my life depended on it.

Cheryl Nelson is a Seattle native and Western Washington University alumna. She recently returned to Bellingham to retire. Cheryl continues to substitute in preschool classrooms with the Opportunity Council of Whatcom County. She has been writing poetry for over thirty years. This is her first prose piece.

A Girl's House

Cami Ostman

Morning sun heated my room through the window as I sat on the floor, cross-legged, with my back pressed against my bed. At any moment, my mother would come and summon me downstairs to get breakfast ready. I held my Bible in my lap. Pastor Ernie had given The Book to me on my third visit to his little Southern Baptist congregation months ago, after I'd risen from my pew, walked down the aisle during the singing of *Just As I Am*, and prayed the Sinner's Prayer. He'd said the answers to all my troubles were inside this Book and had shown me a little table at the front with references. "For trouble with love turn to John 5:13." And "For trouble with parents turn to Deuteronomy 5:16."

Trouble with parents . . . he couldn't even guess! Since June I'd been in charge of watching my three little brothers while my mother worked. My stepfather had left—again. I was mostly glad he was gone. Unkind and occasionally cruel, he scared me. But he would be back. He always came back—sometimes the same day he left, sometimes a few months later. Until he returned (and even after he did), I helped with the boys.

From where I sat on the carpet, I could see the doorway my mother would come through and a full-length mirror reflecting my tousled hair, slept-in black eyeliner, and the big puffs under my eyes. How come I looked like I was a hundred years old at only fourteen?

The house was stirring below. I didn't have much time, but having *The* Book with *all* answers was like holding magic in my hands. I knew answers came from books. Last year in eighth grade we'd read a little play-book called *A Doll's House* by Henrik Ibsen. The world opened to me when Mr. Ibsen's character, Nora, walked out the door at the end of the story. I understood why— perfectly. I'd applauded when we read the final scene out loud in class. Our teacher explained that authors can challenge existing ideas with story. Since then I looked for messages in everything I read.

Cracking open the Bible to the index, I turned to "T" to look up "tired." I wanted something I couldn't put my finger on. Maybe backup from God that my mother's expectations of me were unreasonable. (Mom's refrain: I was her "eyes on the ground.") Maybe some authority behind the resentment I felt this morning: that I shouldn't be stuck here as a built-in babysitter. I said a prayer for God to help me out of my trap. Could I have one day before school starts to go swimming? Or to sit at a park and read?

I heard my mother's footsteps and shoved the Bible under the bed. She wasn't a fan of "this church thing."

There was a knock before she poked her head in the door. "Get up, kiddo. I'm late."

"I'll be right down," I responded.

"Now, honey."

"Can Dane be in charge today?"

"Nope. You're on," she said curtly. She sounded irritated.

"Why?" I whined. "He should have to. He's twelve now. He hasn't done anything at all this summer."

"Don't push me," her voice was rising. "You're the girl. And you're the oldest. Boys don't mature as quickly. And we've all got jobs to do. Yours is to take care of the boys. Mine is to go to work to pay for your life. Get down these stairs."

Then she was gone.

I pulled the Bible back out and flipped it open again. Surely God didn't mean for me to always have to be in charge just because I was a girl. I went straight to "W" for "women, the role of."

I found two verses and turned to them quickly:

Let a woman learn quietly with all submissiveness. I do not permit a woman to teach or to exercise authority over a man; rather, she is to remain quiet. For Adam was formed first, then Eve; and Adam was not deceived, but the woman was deceived and became a transgressor. Yet she will be saved through childbearing—if they continue in faith and love and holiness, with self-control. I Timothy 2:11-15

The women should keep silent in the churches. For they are not permitted to speak, but should be in submission, as the Law also says. If there is anything they desire to learn, let them ask their husbands at home. For it is shameful for a woman to speak in church. I Corinthians 14:34-35

What?

I wasn't expecting this. A terrible, startling sense of dread settled on me, and my heart began beating hard in my chest. So, I was right that God didn't want me to be in charge, but He also didn't even want me to talk?!

And, was it really possible that He held me and women everywhere responsible for what Eve did?

I hoped I was misunderstanding something. I could feel panic closing in. I reread the passages, trying to puzzle out what *else* they might mean.

"Hey," my mother was shouting at me from the bottom of the stairs. "Get down here. I have to go." She was past irritation and onto mad now. I pushed the Bible back under the bed and slumped down to the kitchen to take Baby Matt, who was two, off her hands.

* * *

When my mother was gone to work and everyone had Sugar Pops in front of the television, I retrieved The Book from my room and called my friend Suzy from the kitchen phone. She'd started Bible study at least a year ago.

"What's this mean?" Cradling the phone against my shoulder and holding the big Bible open with both hands, I read her the passages. I whispered so my brothers couldn't hear. I glanced at them. Chad, nine, was trying unsuccessfully to shoo baby Matt away from blocking the television. Matty, dressed in nothing but his diaper, kept dancing to the music in a commercial.

"It means what it says," Suzy answered.

"What, like that we can't talk in church? And we have to submit to men?"

"Right. That's why the pastors are all men."

"Why?"

"Because God said." Suzy sighed like she was explaining something to a small child. "Look, it's all right there in black and white. It's part of our punishment for a woman being the first one to sin in the Garden of Eden."

There wasn't much in this explanation to give me solace. "Do you believe this, Suzy? That God is still mad at all women for Eve's mistake?"

"Have to. It says so in the Bible, doesn't it? And that Bible you're reading is God's word. It's got the whole truth and nothing but the truth."

I was silent.

"Listen if this really bothers you, go talk to Pastor Ernie about it. He's always in the office on Tuesdays, I think."

That's exactly what I would do. I hung up the phone, paced the kitchen for a while and then made a decision.

I couldn't do anything else—the dishes, the laundry, even sit down with the boys and watch TV—until I understood if God really thought I was meant to be small and quiet. I thought of Nora in Ibsen's play. She couldn't stand being silenced like a child, and marched right out of her marriage. Was she wrong? I'd thought she was so brave to stand up for herself.

Shakily, I went up to my room and threw on shorts, a T-shirt, and sneakers. Back in the TV room, I told Dane to watch the baby because I was going to take a walk. He glared at me. I didn't tell him it would be a two-mile walk, each way. Truthfully, I didn't know the distance; it only took a few minutes to get there every Sunday when Pastor Ernie picked me up in his shiny black Camaro.

The Book under my arm, I stepped into the August sunshine, hotter than usual for the Pacific Northwest, and started walking. I began to sweat right away, but neither the heat nor any distance would deter me. There were no sidewalks on the busy roads, and cars rushed by as I recited the words from the verses in my mind and practiced how I would ask my questions when I got to the church.

Finally, almost an hour after I'd left home, I arrived at Martha Lake Baptist Church, dripping with perspiration, a tight lump in my throat, the Bible slipping from my moist hands as I entered the building.

The pastor's office door was near the front of the sanctuary, to the left of the podium where he spoke each week. I scarcely gave myself time to be grateful to be out of the sun before rushing down the aisle and knocking at his door.

"Come in," came Ernie's gravelly voice. I crept inside, and he looked up from his reading with surprise. Then concern crossed his mustached face—gray eyebrows bent toward one another. "Are you alright dear? How did you get here?"

"Walked," I said.

"I see. Sit down. What's going on?"

I sat in the chair across from his large wooden desk and wiped sweat from my upper lip. He came around to my side and perched himself on the desk so that he hovered above me.

I opened the Bible. "I read this today . . . What does it mean?"

He took The Book from me and read the verse from Corinthians. Then he chuckled. Like something was funny. "You walked all the way here to ask me about this?"

I nodded.

"You could have called on the phone."

I hadn't thought of that.

"Well, then." His voice was soothing. "The verse simply means that leadership in a congregation should be comprised of men."

"But why?" Again my heart pounded hard.

"Because of the Fall in the Garden, men are designated for leadership." Seeing my watery eyes, he quickly added, "This does *not* mean that men are more important than women, dear. It simply means we have our roles. It is for men to lead and for women to follow with submission. This is God's plan." Then to prove his point, he flipped to the verse from Timothy. "You see, it says, 'I do not permit a woman to teach.' Women can do many things in the church; they simply don't teach. Don't worry. You'll find your role in time."

I sat dumbly. He thought I was afraid I wouldn't fit in at church? I was worried about something bigger than church. I was worried about my *life!* I was in charge of everything, but I wasn't supposed to be. I had three brothers, a father, and a stepfather, and I was the one my mother gave responsibility to. Always. How was I going to obey both my mother *and* God? And then there was the "remain quiet" issue: Of course, I didn't want to be in charge, but I didn't want to be silenced instead. God had me in a terrible pickle.

After getting me a glass of water, Pastor ushered me back outside and reminded me to be careful on my way home.

I stood on the edge of the churchyard. Sad. Ruined. Tears streaming freely now.

I looked up at the sun through a cluster of evergreen trees and suddenly realized I must have been gone a long time. My mother would call at lunch, and if she knew I'd left, I would be in serious trouble. I sped up my pace to as fast a clip as I could manage, sweating again, the Bible feeling very heavy in my hand now.

I thought of Nora from Ibsen's play. I wished I was someone who could walk out a door and never come back.

Cami Ostman is the author of the memoir Second Wind: One Woman's Midlife Quest to Run Seven Marathons on Seven Continents *and the editor of several anthologies. She's one of the founders of Red Wheelbarrow Writers and the CEO of The Narrative Project which supports authors in getting their books done.*

The Bible Thief

Penny Page

Half the size of a deck of cards, the small book fit perfectly into my seven-year-old hand. I cupped it gently and ran my fingers over its pristine white leather cover. Shiny gold letters in fancy script spelled the word Bible across the front. My heart fluttered as I gazed down at this very special book, turning it over in my hand, carefully fanning the gold-edged pages. I had never seen anything quite like it. I wanted it. Not so much because it was a Bible, but because it was such a special book, so pretty and perfect in its diminutive design, spotlessly clean, and glittering with gold. A flawless little package with fully functioning readable pages!

The year was 1963, and back then we had far fewer distractions than kids today. My primary sources of preferred entertainment consisted of Saturday morning cartoons, listening in on the telephone party-line, and reading lots and lots of books. I even remember reading my way through a skinny encyclopedia set that my mom brought home one volume at a time from Safeway—a promotional giveaway if the customer bought enough groceries. Reading enabled me to experience adventures in places far beyond the walls of our three-bedroom rambler. It's also why I was drawn to the little Bible like a moth to a flame. I had to have it.

The Sunday school teacher announced that the little Bible was a prize to be awarded to the boy or girl who answered the most Bible-related questions correctly that morning. Ten questions later, only two of us were left: me and Kathy Magnuson. Kathy was the teacher's pet who always seemed to know everything and do everything right. I believed, though, that the little Bible and I had a connection, and that if God really existed, this time I would win. The teacher insisted that I place the Bible back into the prize box until the quiz was over. I reluctantly released my newfound treasure.

The teacher cleared her throat. "Okay, girls, whoever answers the next question correctly wins the prize." I held my breath and leaned forward, listening hard.

"Here's the question: Jesus was born—"

"In a stable!" I shouted. And then, just to flaunt my knowledge, I added, "He was laid in a manger!" I had won! My heart soared. I was already reaching for the little Bible, anticipating the feel of the white leather under my fingertips, when the teacher held up her hand.

"Wait for the rest of the question, please." She cleared her throat. "Jesus was born in what town?"

"Bethlehem!" Kathy crowed.

The teacher pointed at Kathy. "That's correct, Kathy. You win."

I couldn't believe what I was hearing. "But I was right, too! Jesus was born in a stable and laid in a manger!" I cried.

"Yes, but you didn't listen to the entire question before answering. I asked what town, not what kind of building."

I watched with raging envy as the girl who always won everything picked up my Bible, barely glanced at its unique beauty, and walked away with it in her undeserving hand. I was fuming. I wanted to beat her up, or at least challenge her to a running race, which I knew I would win, and take the Bible as my prize. But at seven years of age, I was old enough to know that such behavior would be frowned upon in Sunday school.

After church, I squeezed into the car with the Bevinson family for the ride home. My own parents never took me to church, but Mrs. Bevinson did. She'd stop by my house on Sunday morning, and I would pile into the car with her three kids for my ride to the First Congregational Church. Lloyd, Ralph, and Patty Bevinson, all near my age, lived about three blocks from my house, an easy walk up an alley and then over a short path to their street. I spent a lot of time with them roaming the neighborhood, tromping through woods and fields, and catching water skippers in the creek. Taking an additional child to church seems like a generous and unselfish thing to do on Mrs. Bevinson's part, but my house was right on the way, and I suspect she figured that if I was going to be spending large amounts of time with her kids, somebody had to put the fear of God in me.

On the ride home that day, I tried to put my humiliating defeat and the loss of the little Bible out of my mind, but the desire to possess the white and shining book was planted deep. I couldn't think of anything I wanted more.

A week later, Christmas of 1963 was only a few days away. The air was cold, and frosty snow clung in patches to the grass. As usual, I was over at the Bevinsons. We were playing inside because of the wintery weather, and that's when I spotted it. Almost hidden and indistinguishable among the litter of toys that covered the floor—a little Bible! I couldn't believe my eyes. I did a double take, and then, like a drowning person to a life vest, raced to it with outstretched arms.

This tiny Bible had a green leather cover, not as beautiful as the white, but Bible was still spelled out in gold script, and the edges of the pages shone just as brightly as I checked to make sure that the inside of the small book contained the same readable print, that this wasn't some cheap imitation. The neat text leapt out at me, complete with number and verse. It was the real thing!

I didn't know how the Bevinsons came to possess this wonderful book; maybe they got it from the First Congregational Church. I didn't ask, and I didn't care. Based on the way they had so carelessly mingled it with the trashy toys, they obviously had no appreciation for its specialness.

I saw my chance. I held my cherished find in a folded hand behind my back and told them it was time for me to go home. No argument or question from any of the Bevinsons. I put on my car coat, slipped the little book into the pocket, and took my leave. The Bible was mine!

Outside it was near freezing, and in my anxious excitement, I neglected to zip up my coat or pull the hood up for the three-block walk. Halfway home my nose was dripping slime and my ears were freezing, but I was too wound up to notice, absorbed with thoughts of being able to examine my new possession in the privacy of my bedroom.

Fifty-four years later, I don't remember what words of wisdom the little Bible contained. Obviously, it was a drastically condensed version. But I suspect the smart money would bet that it included the ten commandments of which number eight reads: *You Shall Not Steal.* At that time, however, the irony was lost on me.

On Christmas Eve day, I was sitting in the living room admiring the Christmas tree lights. The little Bible was sitting on the coffee table in front of me next to a heaping bowl of filbert nuts. The doorbell rang. Who could this be? Christmas carolers perhaps? My mom opened the door and I saw the Bevinsons, their four hulking shadows shuffling around on the front porch. What were they doing here?

Mrs. Bevinson handed my mom a Christmas card. "Thought I'd save a stamp and drop by to wish you a Merry Christmas!" My mom thanked her and invited them to come in.

As they stepped in, I remembered that the Bible, their Bible, was sitting in plain sight on the coffee table. I watched with skyrocketing distress as Lloyd, Ralph, and Patty crossed the living room toward me. I grabbed up the book and looked around frantically for a place to hide it. I saw only one option—the nuts! I plunged the Bible into the heaping bowl of filberts and then piled more nuts on top to bury the small book from view.

Lloyd, Ralph, and Patty settled onto the floor across from me on the other side of the coffee table. They went greedily for the nut bowl, the three of them quickly picking up filberts and efficiently sharing the silver nutcracker, getting closer and closer to the buried Bible with each snap of the shell. *Stop, stop!* I screamed in my head. But they kept cracking and eating like they'd never had a filbert before. Every time they reached for a nut, I held my breath. If they kept this up, they'd unearth the Bible in no time. What should I do? Pick up the bowl and refuse to let them have any more nuts?

In less than a minute, a corner of green leather was poking from the pile. Lloyd looked at it curiously, poked around with his fingers and pulled the little book out from under the nuts.

He scrutinized the small book for a moment and then said, surprised, "Hey, this is ours!" The three of them looked at the little Bible, and then at me, dumbfounded, as though I had suddenly sprouted horns out of my ears. I froze, and my stomach went heavy and flat, like a punctured tire. I was caught. I had no explanation for how their little Bible ended up in my nut bowl other than the obvious—that I'd stolen it and hidden it there.

I don't remember what I said, perhaps I've blocked it out, but they took their little Bible and left. One thing I'll never forget, however, were the looks on their faces. First surprise at finding the book, then realization as it dawned on them that I had stolen the book from their house, and then hidden it, and that I wasn't a person they could trust anymore.

My trek home from the Bevinsons in an unzipped coat, with no hood and a stolen Bible in my pocket, had also left me with a sore throat and a stuffed-up nose which put a serious damper on my Christmas holidays. Perhaps some sort of well-deserved cosmic payback at work. Truthfully, if Kathy Magnuson had been the target of my thievery, I wouldn't have felt so bad, but Lloyd, Ralph, and Patty were my friends. We shared most of our toys with each other; we didn't have to steal.

Reflecting on those days, I've asked myself who steals a Bible of all things, and at Christmas time no less? But I did. The good thing that came out of that experience was that it cured me of stealing. I've never wanted anything enough to relive the panic and shame of that Christmas Eve in 1963—unless you want to count the dress I bought at Nordstrom, wore to a cocktail party, accidently doused one of the gauzy white sleeves in red wine, and returned the next day. But that's another story.

Penny Page is a writer, a reader, a gardener, and a native Bellinghamster. She writes primarily paranormal mysteries, which include her self-published novella Not Haunted, *and three other novels:* Coven Corners *(a PNWA Sci/Fi Paranormal finalist),* Bayview Cemetery, *and* A New Kind of Monster.

The Mason

Jack Remick

So much depends on the tools. A worker without tools is like a myth without a ritual. The ritual drives the work, drives the man to complete the work. As with every ritual, the participants must know not just what to do, but when to do it, and most important, when not.

The farmer who plants his seed in the dead of winter cannot expect to reap his wheat in the August sun.

So it was with the stonemason who came to repair the ancient brick chimney of my house. Time and weather eat brick, eat the mortar holding the brick in place. It was time to smooth the wrinkles of age scoured into the brick, but I did not have the tools, did not have the wisdom, did not know when or how. And so I called the stonemason.

He arrived at 8:30 am on a Wednesday in November. His truck was a tool that carried all his tools—but the most important was the man. The man who knows the tools to use and when to use them. The wisdom is not in the tools but in the man. If the man does not know the tools, the ritual cannot come to its end.

The tools let us see the man as he works. We do not often think of the truck as a tool, but without it, the man cannot complete his tasks. The truck, then, is the tool that takes him to the place where he works at 8:30 am, this man who knows how and when and why.

He brought a ladder. He brought a mixer for the concrete. He brought the right power tool.

"Power?" He asked me at 8:35. I pointed to the power outlet on the lamp post by the driveway. "And water?" I showed him the spigots still under their winter caps.

"All right to mix here? I won't leave a mess."

Work. Mess. If you work, you understand the rituals of preparation. Knowing what to do, knowing the results of the doing, knowing how it ends is as important as the doing itself.

Then from the truck came the tools—the power cord, the grinder, the hoses, the trowels and scrapers, the chisels, and the hammer. The Mason laid all the tools out on a tarp on the cold ground, laid them out in an order because to the workman, the order of the tools echoes the order of the universe and the spine of the ritual is its order. Precision in the tools, as precise as the orbits of moons, as exact as the ellipses of the sun tracking its path through the cosmos.

The Mason then laid out the stainless-steel chimney cap—a tool only he knows how to use, and why. The steel shimmered in the mist of the morning. As with all the rituals we practice, the mystery unveiled is the guide through time.

It is not enough to be. You must be wise. Wisdom is always knowing what to do, when to do it, and why to do it. I think about the story of the railroad worker whose job was to tap the steel wheels of the railcars of the waiting train at the station.

But no one told him why.

Why tap the steel wheels?

Clang. He walked the length of the train. *Clang.* Why? Why tap the wheels? No one told him to listen for the dull thud of cracked steel. A man with a tool—the hammer—but not knowing why, knowing only what.

So, wisdom is not just what, but why and when and how.

I watched the man on the roof transform from a man to half a machine as he donned his breather—a tool that he knew would keep him alive. Each tool has its purpose, each tool has its meaning. I watched as the Mason ground out the grout holding the bricks, grout weathered by rain and ice and snow and heat until it had rotted and the bricks had loosened and in their looseness had become conduits for rain and ice and destruction.

The man with the mask started his grinder—a durable instrument, a precision instrument that he used to bore out the rotten grout, and there was dust.

And the breather, the mask, the life-giving, lifesaving breather was sheathed in a cloud of dust—mortar dust, ground so fine it flew and filled the air and settled into the house. The scent of grout dust has its own peculiar odor. There is nothing fresh about it, but there is, in it, the odor of decay and death.

Tools. Every tool as precise as the man.

Minutes and hours slid by before the grinding fell silent. Then came the hammering. The sound of hammer and chisel. The sound of brick and steel and concrete— the mask, the grinder. The hammer and the chisel now laid aside.

Silence as the man hoisted the buckets filled with sand and cement and water mixed in a machine that until that moment had lain at the ready. With the tool, the trowel, the man filled the gaps he ground around the brick and he built the cap.

He built the cap with thin brick he had cut with the saw. He laid the brick onto the bed of grout and I heard the tap-tap-tapping of the handle of the trowel on the brick. And when the cap was sealed and the mortar set, the man locked the shiny steel chimney cap in place and the sun blazed from it, stabbing the eye with its solar sharpness and he then stepped back to look at his work.

This was the work of a wise man with tools. The right tools for the right job at the right time.

He was done. The work was done. He knew the work was done.

He had done it many times, for many days, for many people, and his wisdom was knowing when to do it, why to do it and when it was done.

The Mason worked with his hands in the sun and the wind. His work was smooth and, in a way, kind, as if he understood the brick and its life and what it meant. His work, were it a man, would be proud that he had done it. The work would tell him, as I told him,

"Terry, you do magnificent work. I am happy and I am proud to see this work done so well."

He blushed.

Had no one ever told him before that his work was superior? Had no one told him that he, with his tools, had cleaned out the rot, saved the decaying corpse of time living in the brick and the moss and the grit?

This man blushed. I know that always before the recompense was only money. They paid him for his time, for his body, for his tools. But more than that they paid him for what he knew. He knew what he saw when he saw it and he read the palm of time and weather and he knew he could fix the ruined and ragged residue of time—that was what he did.

But cash was not enough.

I knew it was not enough.

I have worked with my hands and gotten only cash. I have sweated in the fields and groaned in the packing sheds and I have hurt my hands, scarred my body, worked in tunnels, and the cash was never enough.

It was not enough. And that was why I told the man with the tools that his work was fine work well done. But the wisdom of work, like all wisdom, is temporal. There will be a time when the Mason will not go onto the roof with his tools because what he knows will no longer be needed.

Steel and glass take the place of brick and grout and the man's wisdom will die with him. The wisdom of work will be silent and there will be no one to pass the knowledge to. Yes, wisdom is knowing what to do, when to do it, why to do it, and the last, the very last thing is to know what is no longer needed.

So it was with this Mason.

As I looked at his work, I saw the wisdom that goes back in time to a time when the placement of hod was an art.

You see that art today in the older buildings, scarred and living past their time. You see rows of soldiers, the side-by-side thin brick at attention, and you see the sailors wide and side-by-side, and you see the courses stacked up, you see the art and you see where the wisdom of the Mason came from and you imagine the end of wisdom.

All his secrets will die the day those buildings come down.

He said to me, as he washed and dried his hands to flush away the residue of his craft,

"Your chimney is over fifty years old. They don't do it that way anymore."

He pointed to the brick now capped with its stainless-steel crown.

"You see? These bricks aren't regular. These are four-inch brick mixed with the two-inch with the square brick layered into rectangles. There is a name for that," he said, "but no one remembers it. The man who taught me—T Bolt—knew, but he did not tell me."

And for a moment I was sad. The waning of wisdom, the dying of an art. I am thankful that the art of his predecessors lived in the Mason. They were men who knew secrets that died with them.

He stood for a while looking up at his work. It was solid work done by a solid man, a fine and good man. He smiled.

He returned his tools to the truck. The power cord and grinder, the hammer and the chisels, the buckets and the mixer were all now hidden in the belly of the truck under a tarp the color of sand.

It was with some regret that I handed the Mason a piece of paper with his reward on it. I knew that his work would last far longer than the cash. My house was safe because he knew how to use those tools that would one day die.

As he climbed into his truck, he said,

"If you know anyone who needs their chimney tuck pointed give them my number."

With regret, I watched this workman, the Mason drive away.

And then in silence, I went back into my house where the faintest odor of fresh grout clung to the air like the lingering ghost of a timeless ritual.

Jack Remick is a poet, novelist, and short story writer. He is the author of the novels Blood, Gabriela *and* The Widow, *as well as* The California Quartet. *His poetry appears in* Satori: Poems, The Seattle Five Plus One, *and* Josie Delgado: A Poem of the Central Valley.

The Ability to Sit

Laura Rink

Four months short of my fiftieth birthday, I sit cross-legged on a firm round cushion in the carpeted room, devoid of furniture, among twenty-four other women and wait to be engulfed by a meditative calm. I will spend ten days in Noble Silence, the silence of body, speech, and mind, sitting ten nonconsecutive hours of each day in pursuit of that state. The other women entered the hall with some combination of cushions, blankets, kneeling benches, and back rests. A few women sit in chairs. I have the single meditation cushion my mother once used. Previously, I sat on this cushion for a total of ten minutes at a time. But still I feel ready, or at least eager, for the sitting challenge before me.

Of course, I'm not at this Vipassana meditation center to excel at sitting. I'm here to see if a commitment to meditation will have a calming effect on my chaotic, ADD-wired mind. But to meditate is to sit, so sitting is key.

Twenty minutes in, the cushion feels like it is filled with concrete. My buttocks ache and my left knee has a sore spot. In between meditation sessions, I survey the prop shelves and grab a half-moon beanbag cushion.

The change is a welcome relief, until thirty minutes into a two-hour session. My hips complain and my lower back grumbles. I quietly shift about for small amounts of temporary relief.

Meanwhile, my mind is having struggles of its own. What was a revelation in the first hour: simply focus on the feathery movement of air going in and out the opening of my nostrils while I breathed naturally, has now become been there, done that for my mind. *What's next?* Focus on the nostril openings. *Nope. Next!* Hush.

I take some deliberate breaths. Deliberate breathing gives my mind something to do, brings it into the present, then I return to a relaxed natural breath. *I'm bored. Tell me a story.* My mind is here, in the meditation hall, but it also flips through the past and dreams about the future. This cacophony of musings is normal, but distracting me from the task at hand. Nostril openings. *Breath flowing in and out.*

By day two, my butt aches continually as I try three different cushions and my knees groan when I sit cross-legged. I revisit the prop shelves and choose a kneeling bench—my shins under a small slanted table of wood, pillow on top for my butt, folded blanket to pad my knees. Back upright, core firm, hands resting on my thighs. This is my meditative pose, and I set about persevering in it. In my room, on my top bunk, I rotate through a variety of positions but in the hall, I use my kneeling setup, left in place with everyone else's version of sitting nirvana.

Three times a day there are opportunities for walking outside in the chilly autumn, and walk I do, bundled up in layers against the frosty mornings and brisk evenings. Noontime often finds sunshine on the trails that wind around an open meadow and through a Douglas fir forest. I stand with my face in the sun, I do some standing yoga poses, I walk. I want to ask the other women: how are you doing all this sitting? But we can't talk. We are alone, together. At night, I collapse into my bed, horizontal the only position I can master.

Lights come on at 4:00 am. I creep out of my bunk, muscles grateful to be moving but sore nonetheless. I shuffle to the bathroom and splash water on my face. Four thirty to six thirty is the first meditation session, location a choice: either in the hall or in my room. I remain in my room, perched on my bed where I can lean against the wall, rearrange my legs, even stretch out briefly before sitting upright again. I focus on the flutter of air going in and out my nostrils. Then my mind starts up. *I'm bored. BORED!* Like a toddler, my mind cycles this refrain over and over during the next two hours.

The breakfast gong sounds at six thirty—*coffee!* My stiff muscles lower me out of the bunk. There is an hour-and-a-half break before the next meditation session. I remain standing while I eat. I try to eat mindfully, tasting the cinnamon and the honey in the oatmeal, relishing the crunch of apple, the warmth of coffee, but my body urges speed. Soon it will be time to sit again. In a few minutes, I am suiting up to walk in the dissipating dark, first on the gravel driveway, and then, as they become visible, the forest trails.

Every evening from seven to eight fifteen, in the hall, we listen to a recording of the meditation teacher S.N. Goenka. He presents the day's lesson and meditation technique, which we then practice for forty-five minutes. Each new technique continues to be a revelation, or at least something different for my mind to contemplate and my body to practice.

During the one-hour group meditation in the hall, the kneeling bench seems to work for me. I make small adjustments, and then a muscle spasms in my back. I reach my hand around and massage the tight muscle. My core is straining to keep me upright—I slouch and then straighten up. I breathe deliberately. We are not supposed to sit in pain, discomfort yes, but not pain. I thought my body could do this.

Day four is Vipassana Day. The attention on breath has been practice, to calm and focus our minds, and my mind does seem less a whirlpool of clamoring thoughts, if still a coursing river. My body, when not struggling to sit, feels grounded. Today we learn the actual meditation technique. Vipassana means to see things as they really are. We observe the sensations in our body, bit by bit, head to toe and back again. This is different. *A bit tedious.* But also illuminating, the openness of some parts, the thick congestion of others. I linger on a pinched back muscle, use my breath to try to relax it, and that pause in forward motion is my mind's cue to wander—*coffee! hot shower! full body massage!* and whine—*this is hard . . .* and finally continue its often-interrupted journey down my body.

Day five is better, and worse. From nine to eleven, I meditate in my room, shifting positions endlessly, my mind badgering—*tell me a story.* During the two-hour lunch break, I walk and stretch and rest briefly in my bunk. That afternoon, I kneel immobile for one hour, my mind parsing my body piece by piece, observing without judgment. There is a pleasant sensation of vibrations on and under my skin. My mind is focused—*I'm doing it!*—then shifts its attention away from my body—*my cat must be missing me.* I try not to rejoice at the focus or be dejected by the distraction, to not crave or have aversion—the two sources of all suffering we are told: to want what you do not have and to not want what you do have.

In the evening, my body feels warm. I wear my lightweight sweatpants and push up my sleeves while everyone around me is wrapped in silk scarves and wool blankets. During meditation in the hall, I feel a little nauseous and flushed.

Day six. I am feverish. *Let's go home.* An enticing thought. My body shivers. I whisper my predicament to the women's coordinator and ask for a backrest. As soon as I sit down, I cry. My body's relief is profound. I still need cushions for my bottom and back, but now have a support I can relax into. *Fine, we'll stay.*

During the hour-and-a-half meditation after lunch, I nap in my room—I want to be well. Afterwards, I put the backrest in my spot in the meditation hall with the two cushions. My body's solace continues. But my mind? Each meditation session in the hall ends with recorded chanting. During the afternoon session, my mind pleads, *for the love of Buddha, start chanting!*

Which is not practicing the equanimity we've been taught: maintaining a mental calmness in the face of difficult situations or unsettling sensations. Is mental equilibrium even a reasonable goal for me? *Nope.* But that is why I am here, sitting with the discomfort of my body and my mind, to see if I can be a calmer presence in the world. I want to be calmer. *Boring.* Hush.

On day seven, I continue the improvements to my new sitting configuration. I build two pyramids of rolled blankets to support my crossed legs, add another cushion under my tush, and another to better support my back. With all that, I cease performing triage on my body every time I rise from a meditation session. I focus more on the work I am here to do—*bit by bit, head to toe, yep, got it*—even as the blankets slink away from me. I procure two large bolsters to shore up the blankets. My sitting setup has evolved from a single cushion into this complicated nest that requires a balancing act to get in and out of.

By day eight, I no longer feel ill, but complaints still rise from my knees, hips, low back. I try not to crave a pain-free body. This too shall pass, I remind myself. Impermanence, as I learned here, means that every state, physical and emotional, shall not endure, only change is constant. I walk. I sit. My body has an anchored calmness. My mind pauses, and then searches for something to latch onto. *Once upon a time . . .* Hush.

Day nine, my body sits motionless, vibrations running from my head down my arms and torso. I don't rein in my mind when it conjures a scene in a restaurant. I become furious at some stranger. The moment this rage manifests in my mind, the vibrations rise like a swarm of irate bees, thick, and loud, and red. Agitation fills my body. I manage to observe, not judge, just wow, this is anger's effect on my physical being. *That was different!* The vibrations settle back but my skin still hums. *Try love.* But I can't replicate what naturally arose from my wandering mind.

Day ten. A subdued hallelujah. The one-hour group meditations in the hall go better in the morning and evening—those sessions are right after walking breaks. My mind is alert. *In a bored stupor.* More observant than reactive. *Exhausted.* I'm glad I came. I'm glad it's almost over. I sit in my nest for the final session in the hall, present, not exactly meditating, but still, in a meditative state. Upon leaving the retreat, the goal is that we will meditate at home twice a day, morning and evening, for one hour. We are instructed to sit in a comfortable position, upright without physical distress. At home, I sit in my overstuffed chair, my back fully supported, my crossed legs resting on the chair arms. For my body, this meditation session is a revelation. But my mind? *Hush! Breath fluttering in and out.* Good job. *Just kidding — tell me a story.*

Laura Rink is working on a memoir about being diagnosed with ADD at the age of thirty-six. She distracts herself from that work by writing short stories, essays, and sporadic poetry. Her website LauraRink.com features an occasional blog and a picture of her calico cat.

Weather Boy

Rodolph Rowe

The first time I took this young teenager out on a lark, I was just looking for a justifiable way to escape— desperate to get out of the office, flee the tedium of church administration. When I got to Shawn's house, I quickly realized he was far more desperate than I was to flee.

He came to worship each week dressed in the same dark blue suit in dire need of a good dry cleaner, white shirt with clip-on tie. The mother and grandmother accompanied him always wearing what was once fashionable, modest 1950s attire—cotton, flower-print dresses, carefully ironed, with petticoats, and pillbox hats with bird-net veils, bobby-pinned in place.

I never asked exactly what was wrong with him. What would be the purpose in that? He provided enough information in the skein of aching desire he wore like a monk's cowl, shy eyes that wandered nervously away from faces, bottle-top glasses, a mouth that unfortunately hung just a bit open, as if he'd had a stroke.

I arrived at his home for "men time," Shawn's phrase, and entered a stifling, closed-up, two-story tract house, everyone evidently gone nose blind, the doggie stink making me have to gulp hard not to gag. He met me at the door. Bowed his head as he shook my hand. Then in a courtly manner said, "Pastor, welcome to our humble home."

The mother, forties, horsey-faced, bad perm, slumberous-eyed, shook her head in a wonderment of disapproval, while the grandmother, an older version of the daughter, stood behind her, mimicking disdain. "He got ready hours ago, and has been sitting by the window all afternoon."

I could see on Shawn's face the betrayal of this public airing of his immense longing. Part of the punishment, I'd come to understand, for needing anyone besides them, abandoning them, and the house of dogs, even for an afternoon.

We all sat down in the living room, mother, grandmother, and Shawn and I. Exchanged pleasantries: Been in this house that long? Really? A new roof is not something you want to put off. Yes, I also have trouble getting my son to cut the grass without badgering.

Finally, during one of the long, empty pauses, Shawn slapped at his knees and speaking in the drawl of a polite cowboy said, "Guess we better be gettin' on."

Once he got settled with seatbelt fastened, I glanced over to see he was trembling. "What's the plan?" I inquired gently.

"I thought maybe we'd begin at the Red Robin, if that's okay. I'll have a cheeseburger, fries, and a Coke. Maybe a hot-fudge sundae. See how it goes."

All had been painstakingly thought through. Nothing left to chance. "Great! My treat," I said, which threw him a moment.

"No, no! Mother says I have to pay part. Chore money. I've earned five dollars."

"Sure. Fine. No problem, Shawn."

Then a comic throat clearing, signaling a critical subject was about to be raised: How was I at video games? Not good? That was okay, maybe best, if I didn't mind watching him play.

So we moved through the first outing, from burgers to video arcade, to short evening walk, and I began to sense in the boy a rising panic. "Shawn, are you all right?"

His eyes rolled away from me. He shrugged, utterly defeated. "It went so fast."

I had moved to the driver's side of the car. "Well, we could go again next month, no problem."

He removed his glasses, turned away, and wiped at his eyes. Gave a big sigh as he got in the car. "Can we do what we did today, the next time?"

"Sure, or something new if you want."

"No! I want to do just exactly like we did this time, okay?" A tone of voice I'd use if I had to plead for my very life.

"Sure, sure. We can do exactly the same thing we did today."

For the next several years our pattern never varied, same meal, same restaurant, same video arcade. If, for you, happiness was so fleeting, so undependable, and you stumbled upon a formula that worked, why in God's name change it, take a chance? Only a fool wouldn't play a lucky hand until it went cold.

One last thing was added to the strict liturgy of our outings. Looking out the window and nervously bouncing his knees as we made our way home one evening early on, Shawn said, "I want to tell you something, but you can't tell my grandmother or my mother 'cause they'll get mad."

I tried to explain that there were some secrets I couldn't promise to keep, like ones that might harm someone.

"Nothing like that. You see, it's the weather."

"The weather?"

"Yeah. I like to pretend to do the weather, you know, like on KOMO. I don't know why it irritates them, but wow, does it! But I like it. Just for fun, you know. I like to do Steve Poole maybe reporting from Stevens Pass in a snowstorm. Not made up. Try to memorize most of what he says, you know, and Kathi Goertzen at the news desk, and it would be so fun if you would do it with me. Just something we'd save for the ride home. Not do it both ways, just going home for a little bit."

"Okay, I guess, but how will I know what to say?"

"Oh, I'll help. We'll do a run-through before we go on the air."

So we did, pitching our reporters' voices to serious and thoughtful, sometimes full of warning and regret, sometimes sunshine and clearing itself, and sometimes doing small, clever jokes for our loyal audience.

* * *

I can still hear his voice—ponderous, confident, full of momentous forecasts, as a trusted TV friend of his Pacific Northwest people. I can still see a soft radiance in his face, the broadcast lights resting easily upon him like a birthright, as he, a beneficent legend, tells the future, makes suggestions about clothing, traction tires, umbrellas, sunscreen, all to keep his people safe.

Always showing all his cards, here was a wobbly boy, famous in his own mind, wearing a heart full of the weather of hope and compassion. Here was a glory of a boy, wanting only to be of service to as many as possible, while at the same time getting everyone safely home.

Rodolph (Rody) Rowe writes both fiction and nonfiction. "The Weather Boy" is the fourth excerpt to be published from his memoir manuscript, Visitations: Postcards from a Life Lived in Search of God's Presence. *This past year he had his first short story published in* The MOON *magazine.*

I'll Be There

Betty Scott

Mom peered at my son in his crib, his hands in fists, arms and legs raised, voice in full cry. "When you kids were born," she said, "I spent two weeks in the hospital. I've never looked after a three-day old before."

"You're kidding."

Mom shook her head. She giggled when she was nervous. Exhausted, I joined in with laughter and tears. I lifted my newborn, held him in the crook of my arm; he wailed. I raised him to my shoulder. Mom handed me his ruffled blanket. We tucked it around his legs and arms and swaddled him. I was her older daughter, with my first child, her first grandchild. When my son settled down, we laughed again with relief, the three of us adventuring into love and colic.

Mom stayed two weeks before returning to her home in California. She was a long-distance grandmother, but throughout the years, our weekly phone chats often nourished us. Until one day decades later, when Mom had moved into an elder care residential house. Gently, her nurse's aide said, "Your mom is too busy dying to come to the phone. Would you like me to take a message?"

I felt unmoored. "No," I said. "I'll call tomorrow."

Two days later, enveloped in sadness, busy as a college instructor, parent, and health care advocate, I woke before dawn. My bedroom was dark and silent. I had an 8:00 am community meeting to lead. My waking thought: *Dedicate the meeting to Mom. Read a poem about her. Call at the end of the day. Tell the nurse's aide that I honored Mom's life. Ask her to pass the message on before Mom dies.*

But how? How does one introduce their mother at a meeting of elected leaders, social workers, school personnel, physicians, and mental health providers? Since 1999, as president of the National Alliance on Mental Illness (NAMI) of Whatcom County, I participated in meetings to prevent youth suicides, decades after my dad folded himself up in his "easy chair," rarely leaving it in the evenings after the day, tears streaming, he learned that his brother, a World War II veteran, died by suicide.

For two days in March of 2006, our prevention program in Whatcom County school districts and pediatrician offices was being evaluated by Columbia University's representative. I was leading the discussion. *How can I bring Mother and the topic of dying into this meeting? How can I not?* I thought.

Grief is like that. We drift into the sea of self-concerns, often feeling like castaways. *They all have mothers,* I reassured myself, *but what does a public meeting on behalf of teens have to do with my dying mother? How is this relevant?* I lay back down. Pulled the covers up. *So what? Who cares?*

Mothers give birth, I thought. *Birth throws us into the cosmos and into human life, that deep sea of blame and reason; shame and praise; sickness and health; hate and love; grief and joy; propaganda and facts; greed and generosity; drudgeries and productivity; cultural protocols and human-made laws.* Nothing in these thoughts could drag me out from beneath the sheets.

Until my alarm radio blasted. A song brought me the answer. Just like that. The Spinners were singing: "Just call out my name, and I'll be around."

I laughed out loud. For in my mother's worldview, there were no accidents. She thought synchronicities were the natural result of our physical and spiritual lives together. Yet when her actions didn't bring happiness, she'd blame our health care system, or her parents, ex-husband, or political leaders. "If officials say your suicide prevention efforts are a mistake, then you're on the right track," she'd reassure me. Until dementia inspired our nonverbal bonding.

I got out of bed and did a happy dance, anchored to the song. In the shower, I hummed along. I dressed in my business suit. I had a plan and an agenda to pursue.

We gathered in the conference room at the Bellingham School District office, seated ourselves around four long tables set in a square. "I'd like to dedicate this meeting to my mother," I said. My words spewed out in a volcanic rush of pent-up emotions, which felt quite unsettling. I blushed. "My mother and I have talked weekly by phone since I moved here in 1990. Recently, her only words have been 'I don't know,' and 'I love you,' two phrases that mean to me a physical self-reckoning with remorse, and a spiritual connectedness. When I visited her last month, I realized those six words are essential to living peacefully beside one another."

All eyes were focused on me. I took a breath. "Last night I was told she was too engaged in dying to come to the phone." I sighed. "I hope you'll welcome my dedication of this meeting to her. She's a former educator, an English teacher, and like us, spent much of her career connected to young people's well-being. Her reading assignments encouraged students to rise above the unkind stories people tell about each other. Her writing assignments helped students transform their joys and sorrows into creative expression. To honor parents and grandparents and our vital work with and for our community's children, I've brought a poem that captures her unique presence."

The room was quiet. I joked, "My mother is the only person I know with one name, except for Cher. In the 1980s, Mother legally changed her name. Jathene is a combination of her given name Jean and the Greek goddess Athena. She chose no last name. She couldn't find one to fit." They laughed. I read the entire poem which begins: "Jathene is not my mother's birth name. / Her parents gave her three names and called her many others. / It certainly took me a long, long time / to call my humming bird mother, Jathene . . ." It ends with recognition and acceptance: "Ja is part body, Thene is part myth. / My mother's name is Jathene."

I added, "If she were here, she would remind us of the words sung by The Spinners. She would tell us teens need to hear: 'Whenever you want me, I'll be there. Whenever you need me, I'll be there. Just call out my name and I'll be around.' Mother would encourage all of us, gathered here, to work together to build a better system, consistently funded. . . . Let it be said of us," I concluded, "that we dared to be a community, collaborating beyond our workplace in order to support and nurture our community's children."

Those gathered knew that philanthropist William J. Ruane, founder of the Sequoia Fund, created the program. In 1992, through his Carmel Hill Project, Ruane also renovated a community in Harlem, brought in health clinics and other service programs, and gave every child a scholarship to the Catholic school three blocks away. He funded an Accelerated Reader program in New York and Louisiana public schools, and on indigenous peoples' reservations. With Boys Town, USA, he funded the research and training to implement various TeenScreen tools, including a screening for pediatricians to use. Unfortunately, without consistent local, state, and federal funding, programs for children and families don't sustain themselves. Our program was held together by the equivalent of Band-Aids, hard work and the good will of school counselors. All the while, I witnessed political colic: fear and anger and what today we call "fake news" creating false alarms, aspersions against TeenScreen leaders and NAMI National. The meeting dedicated to Mother in March 2006 ended with more work to do.

Later that evening, I called the house where Mother was receiving hospice care. I was surprised when her nurse's aide said, "Just a moment. I'll bring her to the phone."

"Hello," Mother said in a weak voice.

I launched into my story about dedicating the community meeting to her, about the words I'd said, and the song that played on the radio. After a year of just two sentences—six small words—she changed her response. Urgently, with great effort she said, "I dddon't . . . know . . . if I . . . ccccan ccccc-ome baaaaccck." An agonizing moment later, she added, "I have . . . bbbbeen . . . here soooo . . . lllong."

I longed to hear a simple, "Thank you," or "That was loving and brave of you." Instead, I took a deep breath, rallied, and said, "I love you. You will always be in my heart and in my memories." Those were our last spoken words to each other.

The day she died, I was unable to cancel my teaching schedule and follow-up prevention meetings. Numbed and distracted, I anchored myself to the clock. I promised to take Friday afternoon and the weekend to catch my breath, to say good-bye to her.

After my last scheduled meeting, I went to a gym to work out. The owner greeted all who walked through the door. Minutes later, she said, "How are you? You looked sad when you walked in."

I hesitated. I didn't want to burden her, didn't want to speak about losing my mother. But she and I were the only ones in the fitness center. As I extended and released the arms of a flex machine, I heard myself say, "Mother died two days ago. We knew she was dying, but it is still sad." I moved to the next station. I climbed onto a bicycle. I pedaled. I spoke about dedicating a meeting to her. I described my surprise by the song that played on my alarm clock radio. I repeated the lyrics. Then I felt a chill; electrical impulses traveled up and down my spine.

The owner of the gym and I became very quiet. "This is amazing," she whispered. "I have hundreds of recordings that rotate throughout the day."

Yet there it was. Synchronized, a remake of the hit song, these words playing: "Whenever you want me, I'll be there. Whenever you need me, I'll be there. Just call out my name and I'll be around."

I spent the rest of the weekend grieving. Inside my house, alone. But unlike saying good-bye to others, saying good-bye to Mother included dancing to The Spinners with a wooden spoon in my hand, singing off-key, as she always said I did, and dancing, dancing, dancing.

Sadly, our local program ended in 2009, the national program in 2012, seven years after Ruane's death in 2005. Then as today, suicides have a post-traumatic rippling effect. Simply put: blame, ignorance, and pills cannot replace education, support, and skills.

After Mother's passing, grief unmoored me. Yet, with biased perceptions broadcast daily, defined as news within the cultural realities of seven billion people whose feet orbit on this planet, each with important stories to tell, I find strength in "I don't know" and "I love you." I trust in the spirit and power of maternity, the mystery of synchronicities, and love's refrain: *Just call out my name and I'll be around.*

Betty Scott's writing adventures began at The Wenatchee World. *She enjoys editing her daughter's novels, as well as manuscripts by peers. She is writing a third collection of poems and working on a memoir. She and musician J.P. Falcon Grady offer an open mic on Wednesdays at Greene's Corner in Bellingham.*

Keeping Frannie

Judy Shantz

My mother had been christened Frances but a nurse-maid liked to call her Frannie and the name stuck. She had once been Frankie to my father's Johnny, and sometimes even Francesca, but now, all these years later, when my father was no longer alive and the friends were all long gone—the ones who called her Fran—she was, again, simply Frannie.

I sometimes had to try to explain my mother to my friends. I think it was contrast that puzzled them. How could a tall, awkward girl whose clothes always seemed too big and too small at the same time, be the child of this tiny, immaculate woman with a compact gymnast's body?

She wasn't dry and stern and moralistic like some of the other mothers on our street. But neither was she the kind who wanted every kid on the block arriving uninvited and creating havoc in her kitchen. She was always smiling and polite, but quite private.

I see her walking down the upstairs hall, brunette curls framing the heart-shaped face, pretty pink angora sweater over a bottle-green velvet skirt—off to a

Christmas party. I was starstruck. To my seven-year-old eyes she looked perfect; was perfect!

Her worldview was her own creation, spun from her quiet intellect as whole cloth and nothing like what I heard from the other adults in my life. Yes, it was important to learn which fork to use for the salad, but more important was knowing that good manners meant making other people feel comfortable. Yes, it was fun and stirring to go to a parade and wave your flag, but real patriotism meant working to make your community a better place. Her core value was absolute honesty and she answered every question I ever asked her as factually as she could. I was so proud to have her as my mother.

Although she did angrily berate my father when he tiptoed in late, night after night—outside our home no one would ever know. Out there, in the wide world, she was my perfect mother. If she had had a motto, it would have been, "Never make a scene."

So, if that was my mother, who was the screaming harridan in the backseat of the car as my exhausted husband tried to negotiate the streets of Naples in the middle of the night?

Of course, we had suspected. But we had all become experts at rationalizing. The strange tales? Probably bad dreams. The occasional fits of pique? Possibly a lack of sleep. Her decision to take a veritable Imelda of shoes, and only shoes, for a trip back east? Maybe confusion was just a symptom of her loneliness. We had not been schooled in this disease just yet and we had certainly never heard of sundowning.

And so, in spite of these portents, when she suggested that we escort her to Italy for several weeks, we thought we could make it work. Her behavior might be a bit erratic, but she wanted to travel so badly. How could we refuse?

It started well—she was bubbly with excitement when we met at the airport in Richmond that morning. She took the multiple delays in stride, even though she had to sprint through Gatwick to catch the last flight to Naples. But her fatigue was showing when we touched down, six and a half hours later than scheduled, and just as all the car rental agencies were closing.

A very reluctant agent grabbed a key, closed the shutter on his kiosk, and walked us to a parking lot two blocks away. He clicked the key fob and we saw the running lights of a car flash. "That one's yours," he said as he tossed my husband the key and walked away.

The car was so tightly parked that we could not open the hatch to stow our luggage. As my husband attempted to ease it out, he discovered that the gears were stiff and balky, especially reverse.

From then on the tragicomedy of our navigation around Naples unfolded.

"I think we should have turned back there." I was supposed to be the navigator.

"Now is not a good time to tell me. Where can I get off and turn around?"

"What did that sign say?"

"A1, I think."

"Sheesh," I gasped. "It's the Autostrade to Rome. How the hell did we get here? Quick—see that gap in between the cement blocks? Make a U-ee!"

"Where the hell are you taking me?" shrieked our backseat driver. "Where's the hotel?"

The sun had long gone down and Mrs. Hyde was starting to emerge.

"Sorry, Mum. We got off on the wrong road."

"I thought you had been to Italy before. How could you take the wrong road?"

"I have never been to Naples, Mum," I said calmly and reasonably and ready to kill. I glanced at my husband, white-knuckled as he made the illegal U-turn—checking his mirror as he watched for carabinieri, thinking about Italian jails and crossing palms with a few euros.

In the end, we were saved by the police. We had escaped the toll road but managed to get lost on a long, narrow, dead-end street, dark as a coal mine and probably twice as dangerous. In trying to execute a K-turn, reverse gear announced that it had done quite enough for one night. In desperation, my husband put the car in neutral; we jumped out and pushed it backward a few inches, got back in to turn the wheels and inch forward a few inches, over and over again. All the while, there was a mad woman screaming in the backseat. But we got out of there fast. *Varoom!*

"Wheeee," yelled the woman in the backseat.

"Look, police up ahead. It looks like they're questioning a bunch of teenagers."

My husband pulled up and stopped just short of the cops. "You're on," he said.

Any facility with foreign languages abandoned me. "*Scusi, Signore . . . inglese?*"

"No."

"We're lost . . . *siamo.*" I grabbed a word from Spanish and changed a consonant. "*Siamo perditos.*" I thought I might have just said that we were doomed souls, rather than we were lost tourists, but it was worth a try, especially since I was stabbing at a street map of Naples with my finger.

"*Non capisco.*"

Then, *un miracolo*—the other cop swaggered over and said in a carefully cultivated Brooklyn accent, "You from Noo Yawk?" Too many gangster movies, I thought.

The potential arrestees were now forgotten and they stood off by themselves, muttering and sharing a cigarette. The *non-capisco* cop wasn't too happy about the turn of events but the New York cop was in his element. After he told me about his cousin in New York, about working the docks there years earlier, and about having to come back to Naples to look after his old parents, we finally got the conversation back around to us, the lost tourists.

He became galvanized. He gave rapid instructions to his partner. When one of the offending teenagers tried to speak, he waved the boy away. He looked at my map and the hotel address, jumped in his old, pale blue Fiat police car, turned on his single blue flashing light and made a gesture that surely meant "follow us." And follow we did!

Mother was back in full form. "See," she yelled at my husband. "I told you she could speak Italian."

The police took off and roared up the onramp of the *Tangentiale*, a toll road that crosses Naples on a diagonal. New York cop leaned out and said something into the speaker and the crossing arm went up. He roared through but the crossing arm came down in front of us. More panic—we had no coins. But the cop stopped, ran back, and said something into the speaker again. We were back in the chase. Such a strange reversal—chasing the police at freeway speed and with every other driver choosing to fall in behind us. The Keystone Cops do Naples.

"Wheeeeeee!" Mother screeched gleefully from the backseat. "Catch him! Catch him! Go faster!" If she had been a cocker spaniel, she would have had her head out the window with her ears blowing in the wind.

We did eventually get to our hotel, but not before the police themselves got lost and had to phone for help. The kind innkeeper was waiting outside for us and helped my husband and the police push our car into a little courtyard. He showed us to our rooms and handed us a half bottle of wine from his own family's dinner table. We drank it quickly and Mother, crumpled on the bed with a silly grin on her face, called for more.

Next day began the journey. Not just the Naples, Sorrento, Rome, Tuscany journey—but the six-year-long journey of Losing Frannie.

"I remember this road."

"You do, Mum? When were you here?"

"I think I was here with your father."

"That would have been a long time ago then."

"Yes, yes it was." Quite emphatic—then, "No, it wasn't. I was here a couple of months ago."

"A couple of months ago?" I nearly shouted. I had not learned how to play this game very well yet. Were there any rules?

"Yes, I came with the girls from the Senior Centre. We had such a nice day."

The Senior Centre? Incredulity kept me from countering that statement. I looked sideways at my husband.

He was wide-eyed and his breathing was shallow. Panic was going to rule another day!

Yet it really was a lovely trip. Most of the time Mother was Mother, interested and engaged. We toured Pompeii and the Roman Forum. We ate gelato in Siena and bread soup on the Chianti Road. But at least once a day, we were given a glimpse of what was coming.

Out of nowhere one evening, she said, "I am really mad at both of you."

"Why, Mum? What did we do?

"You're always making me eat spinach. You know how much I hate spinach."

"Mum, we're not eating spinach. What are you talking about?"

"I have a good mind to just get on a plane and go home right now. How could you treat me so badly?"

When I was a child I would occasionally be treated to a couple of sugar cubes with my tea. Sometimes I would pour a little tea into the saucer and set my sugar cubes just at the edge, waiting and watching as the dark liquid infiltrated the sugar, staining it, dissolving it, until finally there was nothing left but a slushy pile. This is what I was watching now: little pieces of Frannie, dissolving.

In the Memory Care Unit a few years later, I asked, "Remember when we took the boat back from Positano, Mum? And the loudspeaker played *Return to Sorrento* over and over again?" A moment of uncertainty on her face and then brightly, "And that nice man bought me ice cream." I brighten too. She *has* remembered. I don't add that the "nice man" is her son-in-law. I hum a few bars of the song and the smile stays on her face for a little while. Then the eyes empty once more. I knew it was the last time. They would never fill for me again.

My sisters and I each hold our own versions of these years, similar, but different.

It's up to us now to be keepers of those memories. I must hold in my own memory my mother's honesty and her careful ways. I must remember the taste of gelato in Siena and which fork to use for salad and the musical boat ride from Positano—if I am to keep from forever losing—Frannie.

Judy Shantz is an aspiring writer who has been living and working in Bellingham most of her adult life. Retirement has now given her the opportunity, not only to work on the fiction writing that she loves, but also to explore other genres, especially memoir and essay.

Sharing Stories

Jessica H. Stone

I met a woman in a forest, in Maine, in the autumn of my forty-fifth year. On a three-week break from work, I had traveled east to escape the noise and crowds of southern California, and to outline a novel. I'd rented a drafty cabin lacking in the basics of heat and running water but rich in views and solitude. The cabin came equipped with a hand-pump and a propane stove—the front yard offered a fire pit and a lean-to stacked with dry wood. Too cold now, for tourists, the cabin was mine for thirty dollars a night. I liked everything about the place except the spider and tick-infested outhouse that squatted twenty yards behind the dwelling. To be safe, I never relieved myself without first banging on the wooden seat with a fat stick.

I wore fleece sweats continuously, drank bottomless cups of tea, and wrote in a leather-bound journal. During the day, I listened to the jackhammers of woodpeckers and watched leaves of red, and yellow, and chestnut brown float to the forest floor. At night, I listened to the crackling of burning logs and watched demons and angels twine in dying embers.

Idyllic, meditative, Zen-like. Still, I am basically a city person and so every other day, when the peace and quiet became oppressive, I ventured into town, ordered a salad and coffee at the only café and chatted with locals.

I had not expected to make friends during this trip as I had assumed that people who live in remote, rural areas would be standoffish and suspicious of strangers. And I suspected they might be dull and lacking in social skills. But I soon learned that wasn't the case. The folks I met were friendly and curious. They wanted to know what I did for a living, and why anyone would spend a vacation in an unheated cabin instead of taking a room at one of the big resorts on a waterfront like Rockport or Bar Harbor.

I shared my stories: told them about my day job, and how I was writing a book, and how I thought the idea of quiet time in a secluded cabin would be good for my creative process. They shook their heads and grinned and if they thought I was slightly nuts, they didn't say it.

One afternoon, a new friend—the owner of the butcher shop—offered to bring a bundle of his famous homemade reds out to the cabin after he closed for the day. He said we could stoke up the fire pit and, "have us a hot dog roast."

A far cry from my gluten-free, whole food diet, but it sounded like a culinary adventure too interesting to pass.

We skewered the chunky franks, held them over flames until they sizzled and split, smothered them with whiskey-flavored mustard, and between us, gobbled down a dozen or more. Salty, fatty meat. Then we melted chocolate bars between gooey marshmallows and graham crackers and we passed a bottle of cheap rum. We talked about the town, his ex-wife, my ex-husband, and life in general. I kept mental notes; what a fun passage, I thought, for a travel story.

A quarter moon peeked through the forest's canopy when my buddy finally backed his pickup truck over the gravel driveway and made the turn toward town. I sat alone. The fire dimmed, my breath crystalized.

Sometime in the middle of the night, my body revolted. Everything I'd ingested, liquid and solid, during—seemingly—the past decade, rushed from inside to out, using multiple orifices for escape. My airways filled with vomit. Tangling in my pants, I soiled them. I felt sure I would die. I wanted to die.

I crawled, puking, on hands and knees down the forest path to the outhouse. No fat stick this time. I didn't care; death by brown recluse would be better than this.

She found me in the morning, exhausted, naked from the waist down and covered in my own spew. I hadn't been able to climb the three stairs to the cabin, I lay clinging to the bottom step.

"Ah, Honey." Her voice, deep and throaty, gurgled through my fog. "You musta been eating some of them reds." She scooped me up. I vaguely remember pulling on my filthy sweats and the ride in her car—a vehicle cramped with damp, yellowed newspapers and fast-food wrappers. I sat ankle deep in crumpled cigarette packages, shivering. Frigid morning air squeezed around a plastic sheet duct-taped to the place on the driver's side where window glass should have been.

She helped me up two aluminum steps and into her trailer and then she peeled off my reeking clothes and pushed me into a shower. Gripping a pair of pliers, she turned the stubs where handles used to be. I remember turquoise-green corrosion around the stubs. I remember the metallic-like spikes of hard water. I remember the tangy smell of Lifebuoy soap. The water pressure slowed when she started her washing machine and the temperature shifted from scalding to glacial.

Wrapped in a scratchy wool blanket, I sat next to an electric floor heater and sipped something that tasted vaguely piney, slightly licorice. Cigarette smoke circled her single-wide, my eyes burned, and my head throbbed, but I was warm and I knew I'd live.

My rescuer wore tight jeans tucked into black cowboy boots and a white tee under a plaid flannel shirt. Her silver hair hung in a single braid that swung, rope-like, as she paced the trailer. She talked on the phone.

"I told ja, Dwayne, don't worry. I'll be there in a couple a hours. I'll get 'em all done. Ain't like we got the Shriners commin this weekend." She hung up, grinned at me and twirled one knotty finger next to her temple. "Dwayne, what a spaz. Y'ad think the Shade was a five star or somethin."

The Lazy Shade was the largest motel in the area—twenty rooms. I asked if she was the manager.

She burst into the grating raw laughter of someone who's smoked too many cigarettes and survived too many years of hard living. "Nope. I clean other people's toilets." She struck a wooden match on the stove, held it between shaking fingers, and stared at the flame for a moment. "Funny, the stuff people put in toilets." She lit a cigarette, took a long drag, and exhaled a stream of smoke. She looked at me—waiting.

"Like what?" I asked.

"Like one time I found a lunch pail jammed in a toilet tank. Empty, just a lunch pail." She shrugged. "And one time I found a teddy bear crammed in the bowl soaked with piss." She shook her head then shrugged. "People." She glanced at my now empty mug. "You feelin better, Sugar?"

I nodded.

This time she filled the mug with hot water, added two spoonfuls of instant coffee, and stirred. She handed the cup to me and told me about her second job.

"Ya can't live on what Dwayne pays. Nobody could. So, on Sunday mornings I clean The Big Moose Bar. There's always a fight at the Moose on Friday or Saturday night. Sometimes both." She inhaled then coughed. "Somebody's gotta wipe up the blood and sweep the glass before the football crowd comes in."

She told me about a fight so intense she'd actually watched a wave of blood crest across the barroom floor in front of her push broom.

"That was a good one," she said.

She'd found a gold chain glinting under a pile of broken glass, and using her acrylic fingernails as tongs, she picked it out of the wreckage. When she shook it, a spray of blood and a chip of tooth fell from the links. She soaked the chain in a glass of vodka while she swept the rest of the room. This, she reasoned, would sterilize the gold in case it had any AIDS on it.

"I was gonna pawn it in town. It was heavy; figgered I could get at least a month's rent for it." She smiled and sighed. "Ever see a biker cry?"

I shook my head and noticed the pain was gone.

"Well, it's embarrassing."

She told me about the biker who'd limped into the bar that Sunday afternoon. He'd been all broken up about losing his chain in the fight the night before. "Said his buddy gave it to him when they were in Nam. Said his buddy was dead." She squinted at me through the smoke. "So, what could I do?"

I shrugged.

"Yeah, that's it. Had ta give it back." She stood and nodded toward the rear of the trailer. "Laundry's almost done. I'm gonna nuke us some soup and get you back to the cabin before Dwayne has a hissy." She refused my offer of payment—said we gals have to stick together.

No shivering on the drive back to the cabin thanks to clean, dry clothes and the warmth of mid-morning sun. No talking either, which was fine by me—I was exhausted. I would spend the rest of the day at the cabin, napping. She would spend it at the Lazy Shade, working.

I stood on the cabin steps and watched as she turned her car around. I thought about what had happened and how I would share the story of a woman living in a trailer in a remote, rural forest, who had been kind enough and brave enough to rescue me, a total stranger, from a frightening state. She had scooped me up, without judgment, cleaned me up without recoil, and gently nursed me back to health. I thought about her stories.

Before driving away, she stopped the car, peeled the tape from the driver's side window, and peeked around the plastic.

"Need anything else, Honey?"

"No," I said. "But your stories, you know—about bar fights and other people's toilets—you should write them down." She laughed so hard she started choking. Finally, she wiped tears from her eyes, coughed, and cleared her throat.

"Nobody would want to hear that trash." She started to replace the window covering, then paused. Ghost-like rings of gray-blue smoke curled in the car's interior. "But," she said, "I got 'em. I got stories."

Jessica H. Stone (Jes) is a long-distance sailor and author of the bestseller, Doggy on Deck—Life at Sea with a Salty Dog. *Her novel,* The Last Outrageous Woman, *won First Place in the Chanticleer Awards. When not sailing or traveling, Jes writes in a cottage by the sea. JessicaHStone.com*

Laying the Foundation

Roy Taylor

Fog shrouded the ravines at seven in the morning. Our truck doors creaked open and Dad, James, and I climbed out onto the broad riverbank, the gravel still dark with dew despite the first shy rays of sunlight leaking over the high rim of mountains. A cobalt blue dome outlined the stark, rugged bowl of snowcapped peaks encasing the frontier town of Valdez. Precipitous mountainsides on the far side of the bay lay cloaked in purple shadow while sunlight crept across the green valley floor. The shallow Lowe River gurgled over a bed of glacier-rounded rock.

Stretching, I followed my older brother, age five, to the water's edge where low morning light skipped off silty gray ripples. A raven croaked. Wheeling seagulls bickered and mewed. I zipped my insulated jacket higher against Alaska's midsummer chill.

"Hey, boys," Dad called, "we're loading the truck over here." We shuffled back to where Dad rhythmically shoveled river rock onto the wooden flatbed of the truck, working the rusty blade through the coarse gravel with his boot.

James frowned. "What're we s'posed to do?"

Dad heaved another shovelful. "Just start throwin' rocks in the back. We all need to pitch in if we expect to get the new church built before snow falls."

"But, Dad," James whined, "there's nothing there but a huge hole full of muddy water. There's no way we can fill that with rocks."

Dad tossed more gravel onto the truck. "I'll admit that's a big foundation hole, twenty feet on a side and as deep as you are tall, but we can fill it in, and we will. Let's see how fast we can finish this load."

James and I picked up stones the size of our fists, heaving them onto the pile. My arms ached, but Dad's shovel never slowed until, some hours later, he glanced at the sky. "Must be midmorning, boys. We'd better unload. This rig is sittin' pretty low on the springs." Tossing his shovel in the back, he helped us into the cab and we inched our way across the shallow ditch to the gravel highway, the heavily laden truck squatting and swaying with every turn of the wheel. After crossing the bridge over the twenty-fingered glacial moraine, he turned left on Alaska Avenue, then right on Fifth Street, which marked the outskirts of Valdez in 1954. We passed the only two houses on the block before Dad parked at the site destined to become Alaska's first Free Methodist Church.

Lifting us onto the truck bed, he shoveled while we boys threw rocks into a wheelbarrow. When it was full, Dad jumped down to dump the rocks into the excavation. We worked until, with a splash, the last wheelbarrow load vanished into the muddy water.

James walked to the edge of the abyss. "Where's all this stuff goin'? The water just swallows it up!"

Dad leaned on his shovel and sighed. "It does seem to go all the way to China, but this is only our first load. Let's drive by the house for lunch before we make another run."

The next day, Dad drained the water with a gas-powered pump, revealing a thin layer of topsoil underlain by silty sand. After we helped him dig a six-foot-deep by three-foot-wide ditch around the foundation perimeter using picks and shovels, James squinted across the gaping pit. "Why do we need such a huge hole if we're just gonna fill it up again?"

"Permafrost," Dad said. "The ground freezes three feet down in the winter, but only the top thaws in the summer. If the soil is disturbed, the lower layer will also thaw. If we don't dig the footings deeper than the permafrost, when that soil melts to mud, this building would settle, and the floors and walls would crack. We don't want that to happen to the church, do we?"

James kicked a loose pebble into the ditch. "I s'pose, but this'll pro'bly take us the rest of our lives."

Dad chuckled. "You remember the story Jesus told about the foolish man who built his house on sand and the wise man who built his on solid rock? Which house was still standing after the storm?"

"I know!" I waved. "The one on rock."

"Right. And we want God's house to stand through any storm. C'mon, let's get another load of gravel. By the time we're finished, this foundation will survive an earthquake."

James' prediction that it would take forever to fill the foundation was close to the truth. For all of July and into August, we hauled load after load of gravel until we had lined the entire pit. Then we started building gargantuan heaps of more gravel and then sand all around the perimeter. "These piles," Dad explained, "are for mixing with cement to make concrete. Four men volunteered to help us pour the concrete."

On Saturday, the biggest man, head shaved and muscles straining the sleeves of his T-shirt, unhooked a gas-powered cement mixer from his pickup. He pushed it to the edge of the foundation, crossed his arms, and scrutinized the piles. "Are you sure we've got enough gravel and sand? We don't wanna run out in the middle of the job."

"Should be plenty," Dad said. "By my calculations, we have twenty-three tons of gravel and seventeen of sand."

Whoa! At four years old, I wasn't sure what a ton was, but I knew it was a lot. I felt a deep sense of pride. My Dad, brother, and I had shoveled every pound of that gravel and sand. Twice. I had helped Dad dig this trench, deeper than I was tall, and line the base with rock.

The big man nodded as he yanked the starter rope and the mixer engine coughed to life in a cloud of black smoke. "Let's git 'er goin'." He pulled a lever and the barrel slowly revolved. My brother and I sat on the log pile to watch.

Awkwardly at first, and then with smooth efficiency, the team of men loaded the drum with gravel, sand, cement, and water, the small engine thrumming and the gravel murmuring as it slid inside the metal drum. Every few minutes they tipped the drum and, magically, concrete poured out into wheelbarrows. They dumped the wet concrete into wooden forms at the bottom of the ditch six feet below the surface. The two-foot-wide by one-foot-high forms, laced with reinforcing steel rods, ran completely around the perimeter of the foundation. As the gray mud slid into the forms, one of the men would jump down and smooth it with a board. The crew sat on the logs to eat lunch in shifts, but the mixer never paused until the job was finished in the late afternoon.

After hitching the mixer to his truck, the big man walked back to the edge of the foundation where Dad was cleaning tools. "I don't know how long we'll have to wait for the Second Coming of Christ, Pastor Taylor, but I reckon this church will still be standing. Good job."

The next morning our fledgling congregation gathered for worship, squeezing into one of the parishioner's homes, children cross-legged on the floor and adults on chairs around the walls. Dad, in a dark striped suit and tie, stood near the door and opened his Bible, the gilt worn off the edges of the India paper, the leather binding draped over callused hands. "Our Scripture for today comes from Paul's first letter to the Corinthians. 'For other foundation can no man lay than that is laid, which is Jesus Christ.' "

His gaze swept the room. "Yesterday was a historic day for this young congregation. We poured the footings for the foundation of our new church. We dug them deep, beneath the heaving frost and shifting sand. We laid them with the intent that this church will stand firm for generations to come. But even with our best efforts, this foundation, this building, will not be our real accomplishment here."

He paused, and I squirmed on the hard linoleum. What does he mean? I thought this was our work, the reason our family came north, to build this church.

"For, however well we build, a fire, a flood, or an earthquake may devour everything. Our only accomplishments of lasting value are those which remain after all else has been destroyed. Only God's love is eternal. As followers of Jesus, the work God asks us to do is to share His love with others, and no better foundation can we lay than the love of Jesus Christ, our Rock, our Cornerstone. His love never fails."

One of the parishioners lifted a hand. "Amen!"

Mom stood, and the bellows of her accordion expanded. Rich chords swelled as she raised her alto voice and the congregation joined in four-part harmony. "How firm a foundation, ye Saints of the Lord, is laid for your faith in his excellent Word!" The room trembled to the bass beat of the accordion as we sang out, "For I am thy God, and will still give thee aid; I'll strengthen thee, help thee, and cause thee to stand, upheld by My gracious omnipotent hand."

Walking home through the misty rain, our family detoured to check the new concrete. I leaned over the ditch and peered down with pride at the solid footings, reaching far into the earth.

"Mom." I looked up and took her hand. "This looks really strong to me. Why did Dad say this isn't the foundation we came to build?"

She smiled and hitched me up in her arms. "I'm proud of the hard work you boys and Dad have done. But, nothing we make of wood or concrete will stand forever. What really matters is that you boys build your lives on the foundation of Jesus' love." She kissed my cheek and we walked home to lunch.

The following year, after the church was completed, we left Valdez. A decade later, on Good Friday 1964, the earth shook, the waters roared, and the old town, built on shifting sand, vanished in the aftermath of the largest earthquake ever recorded in North America.

* * *

A half century passed before I returned to Valdez, summiting the stark grandeur of Thompson Pass with my wife on a bright June day. After skirting Worthington Glacier, the highway dropped into the claustrophobic confines of Keystone Canyon, whose sheer cliffs, sprinkled with glittering waterfalls, traced a faraway ribbon of sapphire sky. We drove out onto the forested plain where snowcapped peaks soared a mile above the valley floor, encircling us like a crown.

"Oh my!" my wife gasped. "How many Matterhorns can there be? I see why your mother called Valdez 'Little Switzerland.' "

Our tires thrummed over the bridge crossing the many fingered glacial moraine, and my stomach knotted. Sixty years is a long time. Would anything be left of Old Valdez but my memories?

My wife first spotted the small sign against the backdrop of spruce and alder. "There. *The Old Town Tour.*"

I turned onto a narrow gravel road marked Alaska Avenue and searched vainly for so much as a wall remaining from the old town. A black bear ambled across the single lane, once the major thoroughfare of a thriving frontier town. Parking, we made our way into thick woods where Fifth Street should have been, where my family had labored for half a year to build the log church. But the street had been erased, the forest devouring everything.

My vision blurred. I reached for my wife's hand. Mom and Dad were right. Their life's work didn't depend on concrete footings. Their accomplishments that really mattered were the foundations they nurtured in the hearts of those they loved, foundations made fast to the Rock, foundations which weathered the storms of life, foundations which endure to this day.

Encouraged by his children to write his childhood stories of life on the 1950s Alaskan frontier, Roy Taylor set out to explore the unfamiliar realm of creative writing, there discovering the exorbitant cost and immeasurable satisfaction of storytelling. When he isn't writing, he practices vascular surgery in Bellingham, Washington.

Trusting Intuition

Kathie Tupper

I am flying cross-country on a quest for love, an online encounter about to turn real-time. I've been searching for Mr. Right since age eleven, and forty-three years of heartbreak and never-ending optimism are coming too. At least online, Jack has the right specs. He's fifty-eight, retired, an avid bicyclist, a marathoner, and a hiker. I have high hopes.

The plan is to spend four days together at his place in Alabama, ninety miles from Atlanta, before I spend Thanksgiving with my son, Kyle. "That'll give us plenty of time to get to know each other, let me show you some good hikes in my neck of the woods." Jack had told me on the phone. "I'll drive you to Atlanta afterward; you don't even need to rent a car."

I am headed to meet a true gentleman!

* * *

"We had a tailwind and landed early!" I text Jack when the plane touches down.

"Already here." He fires back. "See you soon!"

I feel exhilarated and stop at the restroom to freshen up. I check out my new sporty ensemble: dress boots, skinny jeans, and a checked flannel over a teal T-shirt. I'm even wearing new underwear.

I apply lipstick and place drops in my eyes to allow the blue to shine through the red. I sweep my freshly colored auburn hair into an up-do. Could I be *that girl*, the one Jack's profile said he's searching for?

Walking outside, I spy him at the curb: tall, distinguished, silver-haired, a man who could command a room. I can't see the riveting blue eyes under dark shades, but I know from photos they are there. He's sporty in gray Kuhl athletic pants, and a black, long-sleeved Adidas zip-neck shirt that emphasizes a slight rounding of his belly. This sets me at ease about my less-than-perfect physical form.

I hug him tightly and enjoy the feeling of his arms around me. I take note that he pulls away first.

Once seated beside him in the gray Dodge pickup, I'm all smiles and happiness. I want to touch his hand, but Jack grips the wheel like he's a bundle of nerves.

"I need to listen to calming music," he says. "This airport baffles me. Half the time I miss my freeway."

Enthusiasm checked, I sit tight.

Once on the freeway, he talks without pause, but never asks me anything about myself. This bugs me, but I try to stay light.

Freeway turns to Alabama foothills. His home is tucked into a suburban cul-de-sac, his yard noticeable for its lack of plant life. As he pulls into the garage, a stoplight positioned at the end turns from green to yellow to red, instructing him precisely where to stop.

"Pretty cool, huh?" he smiles.

We enter his basement. One room has two kayaks and four perfectly lined up expensive bicycles. An abundance of fishing gear sits neatly organized in a corner. Another room holds a complete home gym: treadmill, a fifth bike on a stand, hand weights, mats for stretching, medicine balls, and an inversion table. My eyes fall on dozens of pictures covering all the walls, showing Jack doing triathlons, marathons, holding huge fish, hiking, and bike touring. Always alone. The place is a shrine. *What is he needing to prove?*

Jack carries my forty-seven-pound suitcase upstairs through a tidy kitchen and comfortable living room with a couch, large flat-screen TV, and his La-Z-Boy.

He shows me his room, where by pre-arrangement I will sleep, at least tonight. He will take the couch. Dumping my stuff in an adjacent room, he says, "I'll let you get organized here," and leaves quickly.

After unpacking I return to the living room.

"What do you want to do now?" Jack asks.

"Walk." I say immediately. "I've been sitting all day."

"You got it," he says. "I know just the place. Let's go!"

We drive to a flat, paved trail that runs all the way to Atlanta. As we walk, Jack says, "We're going toward my university. Did you know that it's *the* top-rated school for Criminal Justice in the U.S.? It's where I got my undergrad and graduate degrees." He details his early careers as a Kansas City cop, and two stints in the Army. Again, he asks me nothing about myself.

Back at the truck, my hands are chilly from the night air. "I've got a present for you," I say mischievously. I place a cold hand lightly on Jack's neck, a joke I've played with other dates a hundred times.

Jack stiffens and shakes me off. "*Don't* ever do that again." He gives me such a hard glance, I recoil.

Not sure what to say, I try to explain. "I'm sorry. I was just playing."

"Well, I am not the person to warm your hands up with."

"Okay," I say, rattled.

After dinner at a local restaurant, he grabs my hand, in a comforting, nearly romantic gesture as we walk to the car. But drops it just as suddenly. There's conflict within him, I can tell. He's a southern gentleman who opens doors for me, but reacts if I get too close. His behavior puzzles, even intrigues me, but it makes me edgy too.

Back at the house, Jack kills the engine and turns to me before we get out. "There's something you should know." He says. A pause. "I have a bit of PTSD from my years in the Army. *If* you enter my space at night when I am sleeping, I will think you are an intruder and respond accordingly." Before I can ask what that means, he continues. "I had a buddy once touch my shoulder when I was asleep, to see if I was serious. It didn't go well for him."

My stomach lurches. "Like, what do you mean it didn't go well? Did you attack him?"

"Basically, yes." Jack answers. "So don't do that. Please."

"I won't," I say.

Am I safe here?

I'm suddenly very thankful Kyle has all of Jack's contact information.

Upstairs in the living room, Jack becomes very interested in channel surfing. I take my cue and prepare for bed. When I return from the bathroom to say goodnight, he kisses me lightly on the lips. Perhaps I've misread the situation. *Is distance his way of being respectful?* I can't figure him out, and I'm too tired to try. I retreat to the bedroom, feeling slightly like an intruder.

Jack rises early the next morning, makes coffee, and puts breakfast items out for me. This settles me after last night's confusion. "Hey, be careful," I joke. "I could get used to this!"

We chat amicably about our hiking plans for the day, television droning in the background. Somehow our conversation turns to writing. Jack has written two novels based on his time as a government secret agent and he's working on a third. I tell him I'm writing too, and for the first time he asks me questions about myself. Now we're getting somewhere. I almost disclose areas of personal struggle that appear in my current writing, but a small voice of caution says to hold back. I don't know this man yet.

As if sensing my hesitation, Jack turns away. "I'm taking a break from this conversation," he says abruptly. "Let's go hike."

I feel shut down, again.

The hike is beautiful, but it's not what I'd hoped for. Jack may live like a metronome, but he hikes like an old man. Cautious, slow, meticulous, perhaps that's how he lives his whole life. He doesn't talk much. To fill the silence, I tell him stories. Epic tales of past hikes, including nearly dying in the Grand Canyon. From Jack there is no response. *At all.* I'm embarrassed I tried so hard.

On the ride home, I raise the topic of dating and relationships. I ask Jack about his previous online dating experiences; he asks little in return about mine.

After dinner, I gather my courage to lay my cards on the table. With Jack on his chair, me on the couch, I turn to face him. "In my world," I sputter, "a man and woman would sit close on the couch, see if there's any interest or spark. But I get the feeling that's not what you want." I watch his face tighten.

He sighs, clearly struggling, before saying, "It's not you. I don't find myself attracted to any women right now."

"Are you interested in men?" I ask.

Jack smirks, emitting a forced laugh. "No, it's not that. It's just the retirement thing. Like I mentioned, I only see myself with someone who's retired. Like me. A woman who wants to travel six months of the year with me, do long bike rides, enjoy life the way I do. It's narrow and maybe impossible to find, I don't know."

"Then why did you invite me here?" I ask, suddenly wishing he hadn't.

"I wanted to see if things would be different. You have many of the things I *am* looking for in a woman. But there's just nothing happening for me. No feeling. Blank. A void."

I breathe deeply. Okay, I get it. There won't be any romance on this trip. Jack doesn't even want me here. Disappointment and anger mingle with relief. At least I know what's going on.

I walk slowly down the hallway, alone, for another night. How will we get through the next two days? Hopefully more sunny, warm hikes will do the trick. Maybe we can still develop a friendship.

SO MUCH DEPENDS UPON... · 285

The next morning, I rise before Jack, making plenty of noise to alert him I'm up. When I hear him grunt, I walk down the hallway, calling a cheerful "Good morning!"

"Morning," he mumbles, looking ragged.

Good, I think, *you* should *feel crappy*. Silently, I move past him into the kitchen. Today I'll take care of my own breakfast.

I stay alert to his mood, watching him cautiously. He comments on the news, the fish tales on the sports channel, and eventually settles on MMA. "Do you like fights?" He asks, not looking at me or waiting for an answer.

"What are you thinking for a hike today?" I ask.

"Sit, please." He commands with his tone. "There's something I need to talk to you about."

Obediently, I sit, alert, facing him, hands on knees. "What's up?" I ask.

"I'm having PTSD symptoms," he says, "and they are increasing. My hands are shaking. I am having trouble breathing. And most importantly, I am finding it difficult to look you in the eye."

Eyes wide, I wait.

"I need to take you to your son's. Today. Soon."

Stomach churning, I try to look unfazed. *Is he going to freak out?*

As if reading my mind, Jack glances my direction. "I'm calm now, but go call your son."

Not trusting his reassurance, I gather myself and stand up. I find privacy in the workout shrine and call Kyle with jittery hands. He answers. "Things have gotten weird here," I say with forced calm. "I need to come now." I briefly describe the situation.

"Come," Kyle says. "I'm here."

Jack is still in the kitchen when I return. "Are you okay?" he asks, meeting my eyes now. Tears threaten, so I look away. His concern may be genuine, but I won't let him know how vulnerable I feel.

I nod. "Yep, it's all good. Let me pack up."

He nods in response. "This isn't about you," he says. "It's me. I'm sorry."

I'm suddenly weary and want to be done. Turning from Jack, I move to pack up the pieces of my demolished opportunity. Head high, shoulders back, I let my solace come in knowing that I am headed to be with people who love and cherish me. Instinct tells me there was no love lost on this man.

Kathie Tupper is a health coach, massage therapist, and avid outdoor adventurist. She details her path to finding inner peace and healing through nature in her upcoming memoir, No Crutches for this Mountain Goat. *Read about Kathie's passions for hiking, overcoming obstacles, and cultivating self-love on her website, Tuppers2cents.com*

Wind

Leslie Wharton

When you arrive at the house, you set to work. First searching through the junk drawer for duct tape, you place notes on the doors explaining to the firefighters how to use the water stored in cisterns. If the electric lines go down, it doesn't matter; the house is solar, off the grid. There will be power. You start the pump on the cistern to make sure it works, drag the gas generator away from the house, and move the propane grill off the deck. You hose down the woodshed and move the outdoor furniture away from the house.

The cats are the number one priority. You find their crate and place a Mexican blanket inside. You pack the bag of cat food as if you'll never be able to buy cat food.

Jewelry and silver, passed down for generations, have been stored in baskets by the door thanks to the small fire earlier that spring. The metal box with important papers is right beside them. You put those in the car.

In the bedroom is a wooden box your grandfather made where you keep your journals. It's heavy, but you lug it to the car. A shoebox, decorated with collage, filled with love letters from your husband, is on top of the wooden box; so are your grandfather's journals. All this written memory is next to the bed to gather quickly in any emergency.

Unplugging the laptop, you shove it in a backpack. You remember your wedding dress, which was your mother's too. Grabbing the hanger, you sweep long yards of lace over your arm and then place it on top of the wooden box in the backseat. You gather photo albums you haven't leafed through in years, and family photographs hanging in the living room. Climbing on a stool, you roll up the Native American rug your in-laws gave you, which Grandma traded for sugar and coffee in New Mexico.

In the china cabinet is your Nana's china. Pretty purple china with delicate flowers, which she bought on her honeymoon. You could pack it in the cooler sitting next to the cabinet, but it might break on the way down the bumpy dirt road. So instead, you fill the cooler with frozen trout. You don't want to have killed a living being for no reason. You carry the cooler to the car. Then you wash dishes piled in the sink. You'd feel ashamed to have firefighters, your neighbors, see the house such a mess.

Next, you pull down the curtains from the windows. Curtains can ignite from heat and burn the house down. Your husband throws tools in the back of the truck; no matter what happens he will have to work.

Because you have two cars and a work truck, you need to make two trips to town to get all the vehicles off the mountain. It is a difficult decision, but after a short discussion, you decide to take the cats on the second trip since you don't want to leave them locked in a hot car.

Driving up the driveway, the sky is glowing orange. Hot orange. You panic. Stopping the car, you go back to the husband's truck. Short of breath from adrenaline, your mouth is dry, you say anxiously, "We should bring the cats."

He logically reasons the fire isn't traveling that quickly. You can't smell smoke, so the wind isn't blowing the inferno in your direction. Not yet. It's still at least ten miles away. The wind is wild, lashing out in bursts like an angry spouse, unpredictable, headed toward irrefutable damage, but still it seems to be blowing away from the house. Besides, there have been no evacuation orders. You start to shake with fear, but you concede to leave the cats for the next trip. Tears stream down your face as you carefully drive the winding canyon road to town.

At the base of the canyon, the police are blocking traffic. Guards are only letting residents by. You ask if you'll be allowed back up. The officer says, "At this point, you still can, but it may change."

Your husband says, "If they start blocking the road I'll drive right through to get the cats. What will they do, shoot me?"

At the grocery store, where you leave the car, neighbors are parked with their horse trailer trying to figure out where to bring their horse. They took nothing else from their house, nothing but the horse. Leaving the car with your most valued belongings, you jump in the truck.

As you head back up the canyon, you call your niece. She asks if you saved the poem she wrote about how much she loves you. You hadn't. Your husband calls the owner of the house he is working at, who is out of town, asking if there is anything he could get for them. They hesitate wondering if it is necessary. He tells them, "This is your only chance. I can go now but not later. If I hang up, that's it."

They tell him to rescue two valuable paintings and their computers.

The guards check your IDs and let you pass. You drive past the road that turns off to your house and continue to the customer's house. Their area is officially evacuated, but the police let you through. You find the laptops and paintings. A child's drawing is on the wall above the computer, and you think to go back and grab it, but just as you open the door, embers, still red from burning trees, fall on the house. Burnt bark and ashes fall too, lightly. Black dust. The heat is intense, an out-of-control furnace. Smoke permeates the air.

The wind is crazy. The sky is glowing red when you reach your house. The first thing you do is fill all the water bottles with water. You could pour water on your bodies if you get caught in flames. Besides, you are thirsty enough to drink an ocean. You put the water bottles in a grocery bag and bring them to the car.

You save the framed poem your niece wrote from the library downstairs. You look lovingly at the books. When you see a book on a shelf, you remember the book. If you don't see it, you have no memory of it. The library is an extension of your brain. Still, compared to everything else, books aren't worth saving. You pillage through the desk to find the bills. Your husband says, "Don't bother, just let them burn."

"We'll have to pay the bills even if the house burns." The thought of figuring out all your accounts overwhelms you. The thought of building another house overwhelms you. You save the bills.

There is so much to lose. You find the little black book with pottery glazes your husband spent decades formulating. From the crawl space your favorite skis. Also, sleeping bags, sleeping pads, a cook stove, and a tent. You may have to live in the woods. You both pack raingear although you can't remember the last time it rained in Colorado. Without saying it, you both reason, if the house goes, you'll move to the Pacific Northwest where it rains. The climate here is becoming unsustainable.

Back upstairs, you quickly grab a laundry basket filled with dirty clothes. This being a variety of clothes you actually wear. You add Carhartt work pants, now thinking you may have to build another house, and shoes. Friends will give you clothes, but they may not have your shoe size. Then you search for your bikini because who wants to shop for a bathing suit. Opening the closet you pick your favorite dress and heels, wanting to look good for your husband to comfort him in some small way.

As you carry the basket to the car, the sky is becoming darker and redder. The fire is exploding. You hear no sirens. The volunteer firefighters are fighting this fire by themselves, and the eye of the fire is too far away. There is an eerie silence except for the wind hollering out of control. Raging. The ground is dry, crispy underfoot. Heat overwhelms you. Hot wind whips fiercely. This time, with this fire, you may lose the house. You feel sadness and panic: a toxic mix.

Going back to the laundry room, you see the family pictures hanging there, ones you didn't want in the main part of the house, pictures of your brothers and sisters at awkward ages, wedding pictures of your parents, a picture of your great-great-grandmother, numerous baby pictures. Looking at them, for what might be the last time, you take only one, a picture of your whole family together when you were a teenager.

Back in the kitchen, you pack the ceramic monkey your niece made after a ski trip where you tore around the slopes, laughing about monkeys and Fred the bump.

You take down the cross-stitch your Nana made. Black thread on cream cloth, encircled by cross-stitched hearts with the saying:

Home is where the heart is friends and loved ones meeting.

Joy is where the home is all ready with its greeting.

You leave the watercolor that says:

Everything happens exactly at the right moment, relax and enjoy the adventure.

You save one teacup from your Nana's collection. Red, laced with gold, it made you feel like a princess as a child. It was the one you chose when she said, "Pick out a cup." And then let you sip creamy, sugary coffee. Your parents disapproved, but she said, "She'll be careful." And you were careful, yet now you are not careful enough to save those beautiful teacups.

Panicking, you look around, you might never see the house again, you can hardly breathe. Your home, your beautiful home, might be lost. How can you live without this house? How can you pull it together? You need to gather everything you can, but what do you really need? You had packed none of your husband's pottery, so you grab a few mugs, vases, a cookie jar, and a platter.

You pick a leaf off the split leaf philodendron plant, the "Carl" plant. Grandma bought the plant for your mother-in-law when she gave birth to Carl. She used to hang ornaments on it at Christmas. Pulling a leaf off the Carl plant, you wrap it in a wet paper towel.

Noticing the candlestick holders that your great-grandfather made from a birch tree that fell in a hurricane, you pick them up. Candlesticks made from a tree that fell in a hurricane saved from a house that burns in a wildfire.

Your husband is hosing the eaves when you receive the reverse 9-1-1 call, "You have five minutes to evacuate. Evacuation may be difficult or impossible." There is only one dirt road out. One way out. Having stayed at the house during three other mandatory evacuations, this time with the record heat, years of drought, a forest riddled with dead trees from the pine beetle infestation, and the intense wind, you know that all that truly matters is to escape alive.

Immediately, without a second thought, you put the cats in the car and drive away.

That night, at your friend's house, the cats cower under the bed. None of you can sleep. The room is unbearably hot, but if you open the window, the sound of the wind drains any hope you have. Peering out, you check the direction the flag is flapping. Everything depends on the wind. Whole lives.

Leslie Wharton moved to Bellingham after losing her home in a Colorado wildfire. She then collected stories for Phoenix Rising: Stories of Remarkable Women Walking Through Fire. *She is proud of being instrumental in securing poets and speakers for Bellingham Women's Marches. Leslie is a Sue C. Boynton Walk Award recipient.*

Acknowledgments

So Much Depends Upon . . . Red Wheelbarrow Writers

You are the creators who come together monthly to share stories, create collaborative tales, and encourage novice and seasoned writers alike. Most importantly, you are the writers who made this book possible by your involvement in every step of the journey.

An enormous thank you to the following members who went above and beyond to see this project through:

Founders—Laura Kalpakian, Cami Ostman, and Susan Tive. *Judges*—Susan Chase-Foster, Frances Howard-Snyder, and Carol McMillan. *Editors*—Nancy Adair, Victoria Doerper, Marian Exall, and Linda Q. Lambert. *Copyeditors*—Andrew Shattuck McBride, Kari Neumeyer, and Laura Rink. *Fundraisers*—Nancy Adair, Lisa Dailey, and Marian Exall. *Technical Guru*—Pam Helberg. *Publisher*—Jessica H. Stone, Penchant Press International.

Thanks also to Chris, Azizi, and all the staff at Brandywine Café for providing space for monthly Happy Hours. Deepest heartfelt thanks to the wonderful team at Village Books and Paper Dreams.

Appreciation to the Pickford Film Center, Whatcom Writers and Publishers, and Whatcom Community College for their support and collaboration.

Grateful thanks to cover designer, J. Allen Fielder, and cover photographer, Jolene Hanson.

A special thank you to the following financial donors who helped make the publication of *So Much Depends Upon* ... a reality:

Nancy Adair, Christine Bostrom, Susan Chase-Foster, Lisa Dailey, Ann Derry, Victoria Doerper, Robert Duke, Margaret & Barry Englestad, Marian Exall, Edward Farrell, CJF, Shannon Hager, Jolene Hanson, Sky Hedman, Frances Howard-Snyder, Peggy Kalpakian Johnson, Laura Kalpakian, Linda Q. Lambert & Amory Peck, Richard N. Little, Cheryl Stritzel McCarthy, Carol McMillan, Kenneth Meyer, Linda Morrow, Marla Morrow, Penny Page, Laura & William Rink, Cami Ostman, Jack Remick, Rodolph & Alice Rowe, Betty Scott, Judith Shantz, Priscilla Sharrow, Marguerite Stanbrough, Roy Taylor, and Kathie Tupper.